PEARSON
PUBLISHING

CW01652388

Primary School Science

for Key Stage 2

Science Workbook 2

Materials and Their Properties

Ted Lister and Janet Renshaw

Illustrations by Julie Beer and Matthew Smith

ISBN 1 85749 288 9

First edition 1996

Reprinted 1997

Published by Pearson Publishing, Chesterton Mill, French's Road, Cambridge CB4 3NP
Tel 01223 350555 Fax 01223 356484
Web site http://www.pearson.co.uk/education/

Contents

1 Grouping and classifying materials

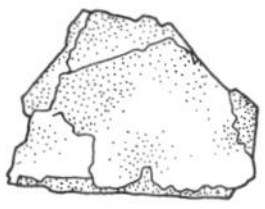

Comparing materials

Everything around us is made of different **materials** which is another word for **substances**. You need to know these words because they will keep coming up. There are so many different sorts that we need to put them into groups, depending on what they are like. We might use the shape of the material or we might use the colour.

Activities

1 Colour in the pictures and circle the odd one out.

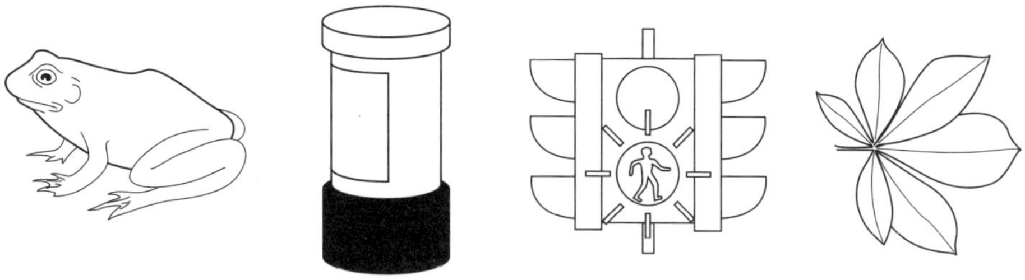

2 Look at the pictures below, circle the odd one out and write down why you have chosen it.

____

____

3 a Look at the pictures and put a tick in the square box ☐ next to all the ones of the same shape.

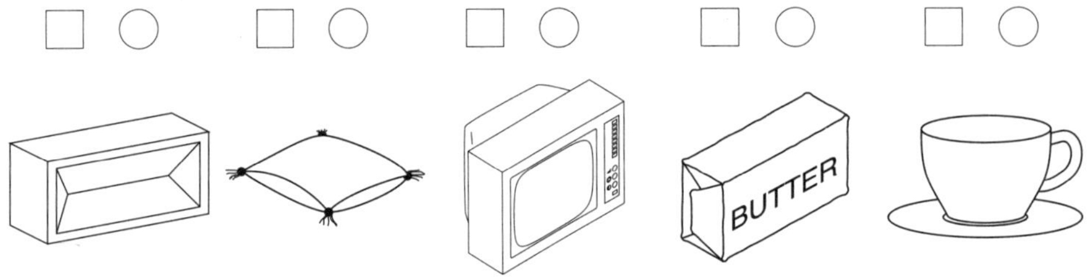

b Now pick out the ones which feel soft when you touch them and put a tick in the circle ○.

c Which one was not in either group?

____

d Which one was in both groups?

____

e Check your answers by seeing if you can make the name of a yellow flower from them.

____

Activity

Look around you and find five objects which have something in common. Add another which is different. Ask someone to pick the odd one out. Did they pick the same one as you? Remember there may be more than one answer.

Properties

A **property** is a feature that belongs to a material. It can tell us about how a material behaves.

For example, all elastic bands can be stretched. They are made of rubber, and rubber has the property of being stretchy.

Questions

1 Write down a material which has the property of being waterproof.

____

2 Write down a material which has the property of being flexible (bendy).

____

3 All liquids have the property of being ____________________.

4 All perfumes have the property of being ____________________.

Materials are chosen for a particular job because they have the right properties. Metals, wood and ceramics (such as pottery) all have different properties. Properties might include: strength, flexibility, hardness, electrical conductivity, transparency, resistance to water, etc.

Activity

What is it about glass that makes it suitable for the jobs below?

____

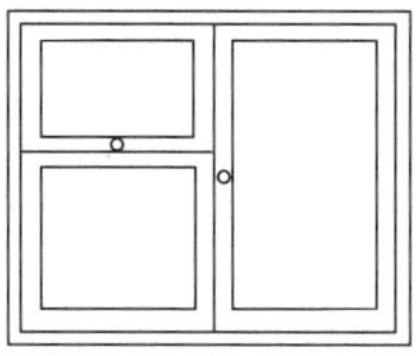

Gold is a metal that is found in a pure form. It looks nice and it is quite a soft metal.

Question

If you lived before the Iron Age, which metal would have been more useful to discover – iron or gold? Explain your choice.

____

____

Activity

Now think what would happen if we used the wrong materials. For example, a raincoat made from newspaper or a hammer made from rubber!

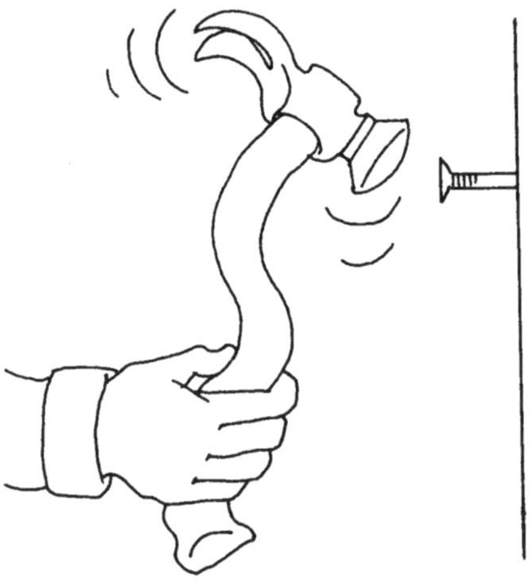

Explain what the problems are in each case.

In the space below, draw two more examples which show where the *wrong* material has been chosen for a particular job.

Activity

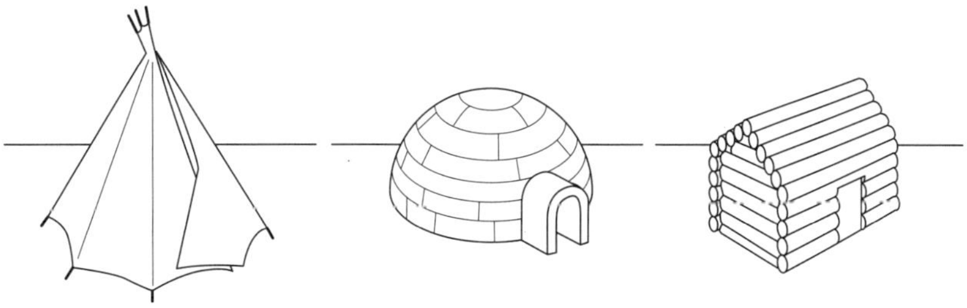

1 List the materials that might be used to make:

- a wigwam ______
- an igloo ______
- a log hut ______

2 Which house would be best if you were moving from place to place?

______

3 Say why you chose this house.

______

4 Which house do you think would be the most uncomfortable to live in?

______

5 Say why you chose this house.

______

6 Which house or houses would be easiest to build from the materials you might find around you?

______

______

Activity

Look at the picture. Below it is a list of the parts of a house. Choose the material which is best suited for each part and the reason for using it. Write your answers in the spaces. You could make a list for your own house too, if it is made from different materials.

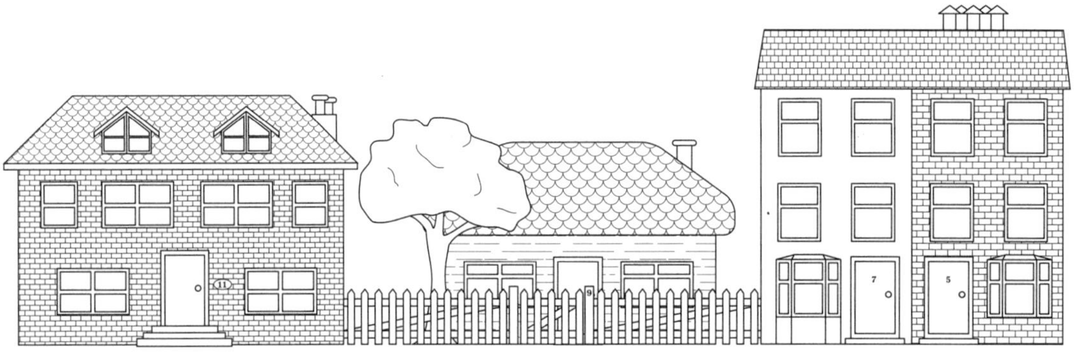

Materials	Plastic Brass Wood Slate Glass
Reasons	Because it is shiny and nice to look at. Because it is hard-wearing and strong. Because it is transparent. Because it is easy to mould into shape and is waterproof. Because it can be painted.

Window	made from	______________________
	why?	______________________
Roof tiles	made from	______________________
	why?	______________________
Door	made from	______________________
	why?	______________________
Gutter	made from	______________________
	why?	______________________
Door handle	made from	______________________
	why?	______________________

Insulators

Have you ever forgotten your gloves on a cold day? If so, you will know that cold hands can make you feel really miserable.

Activity

Which of the gloves would you choose to keep you warm on a wintry day?

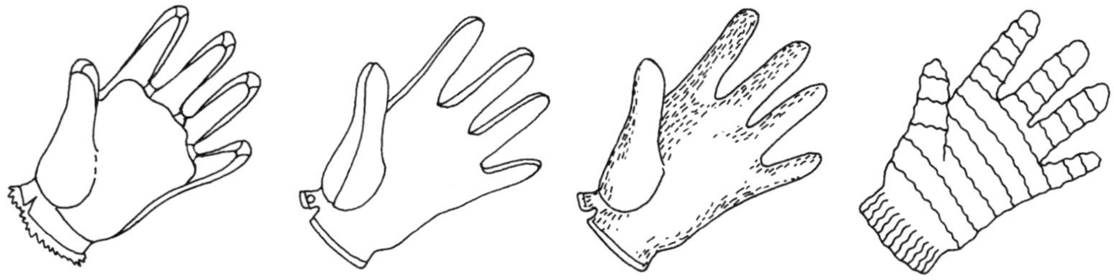

Fur-lined leather *Cotton* *Pile* *Wool*

Think of a way you could test out your answer at home. You can use hot water, tin cans, a thermometer and a stop clock. Write down on a separate piece of paper what your plan would be.

Activity

Find out how the following keep warm:

- polar bears ______________________
- seals ______________________
- birds ______________________
- surfers ______________________

Materials that are good at keeping the heat in are called good **insulators**. These materials don't get hot themselves very quickly.

Activity

For each of the following say what it is, why we need a good insulator, and what it is made from.

a

b

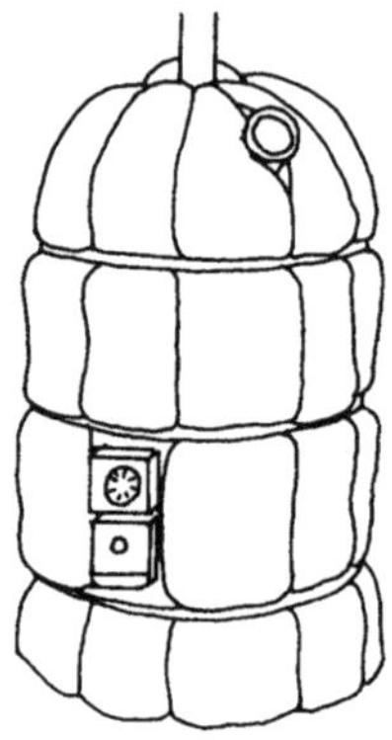

c

a ______________________________

b ______________________________

c ______________________________

Materials which conduct electricity

One of the most important properties of a material is whether it will **conduct** electricity or not. The diagram below shows how we can test this property.

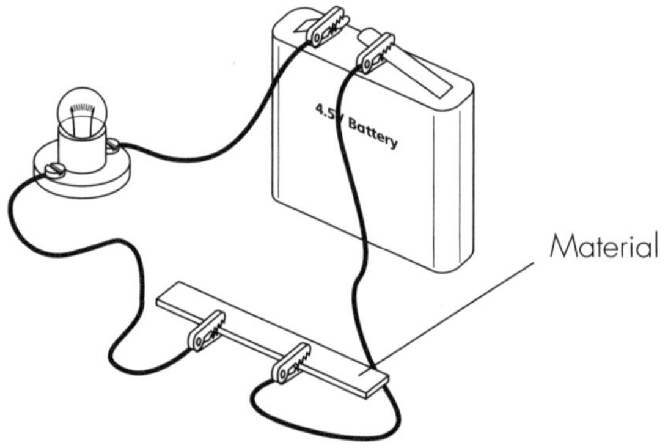

A piece of copper between the crocodile clips will light the bulb, but a piece of wood will not. Copper conducts electricity; wood does not. We call copper an **electrical conductor** and wood an **electrical insulator**. In fact, all metals conduct electricity.

Electrical conductors like copper let us send electricity through power lines and cables.

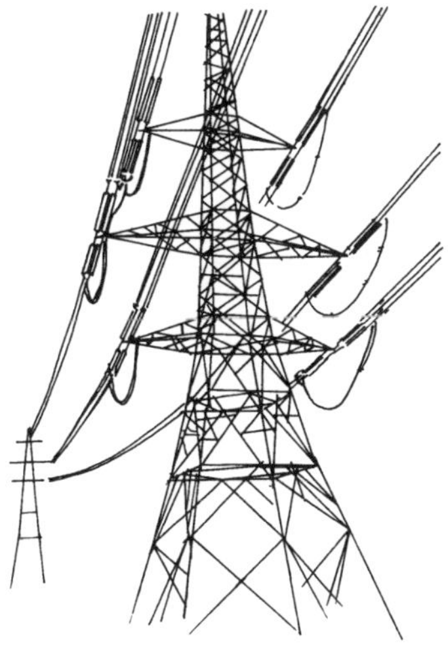

Electricity pylons support electric power cables

Electrical insulators are used to surround these cables to protect us from the dangers of electricity.

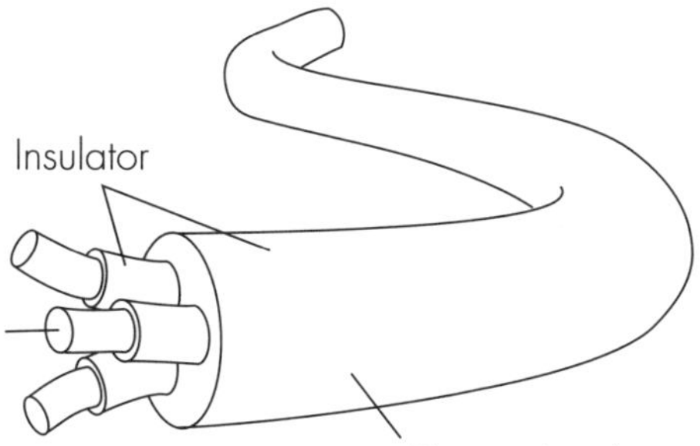

Cables are insulated to protect us

Notice that the word **insulator** is used to describe things that do not let heat travel through them and things that do not let electricity travel through them.

Activity

Do you have an electric kettle at home?

The one in the picture is made of metal, but it has some parts which are made of plastic (a good insulator of heat and electricity). Say which parts are made of plastic and why.

____

____

____

Grouping rocks and soils

Soil is a wonderful mixture of all sorts of things. It began from the rocks around us.

The rocks were ground into many tiny pieces by wind and weather – this is called **erosion**. Air and water trapped between the bits of rock meant that living things could make their homes there. Slowly rock turned to soil. Soil also contains the remains of dead leaves, plants and creatures – this part is called **humus**.

Is all soil the same?

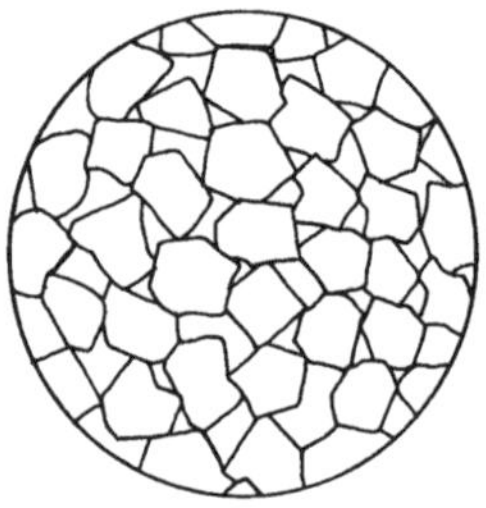

Sand

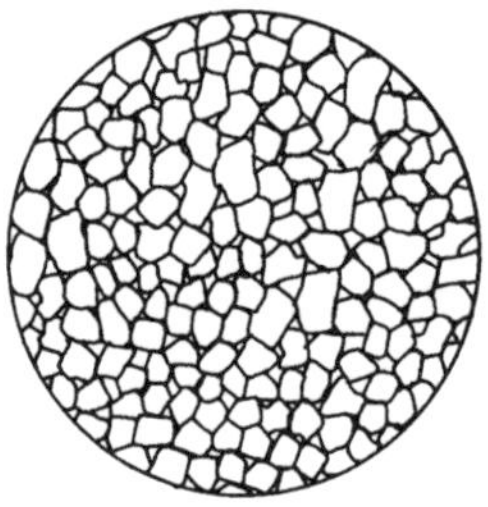

Clay soil

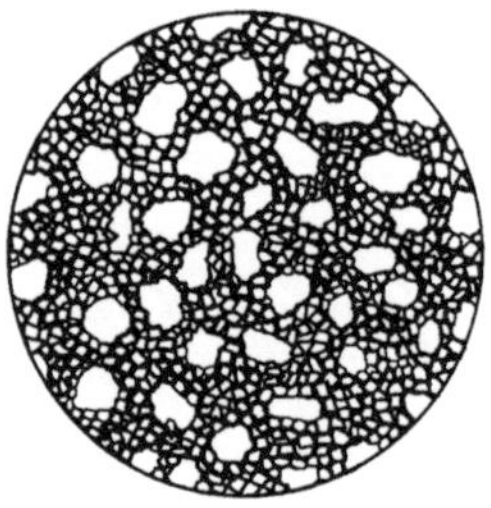

Loamy soil

Find two differences between the soils above.

Activity

If we pour water through some different soils, we can compare how quickly they drain.

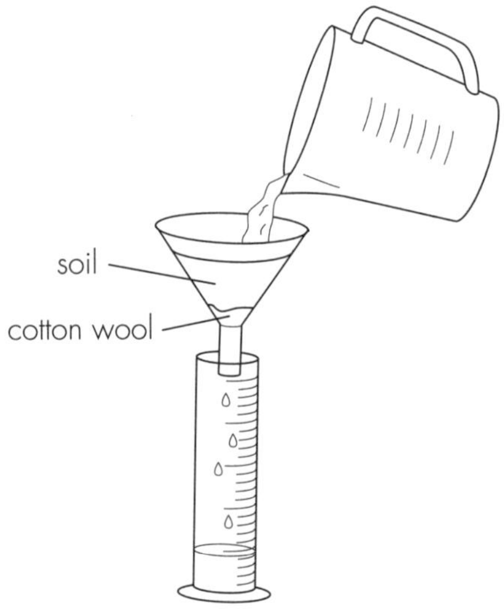

Results:

Type of soil	Time
sand	30 secs
clay	5 mins
loam	3 mins

Which one drained most quickly? ______________________

Suggest why by looking at the soil particles.

____

Comparing soils

One way of comparing soils is to use water to separate the different materials in them.

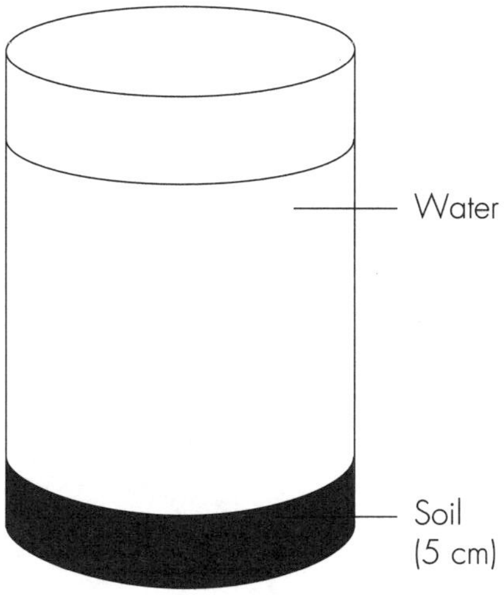

1 Cut the top from a clear plastic bottle.

2 Put about 5 cm depth of soil into the bottom and fill up with water.

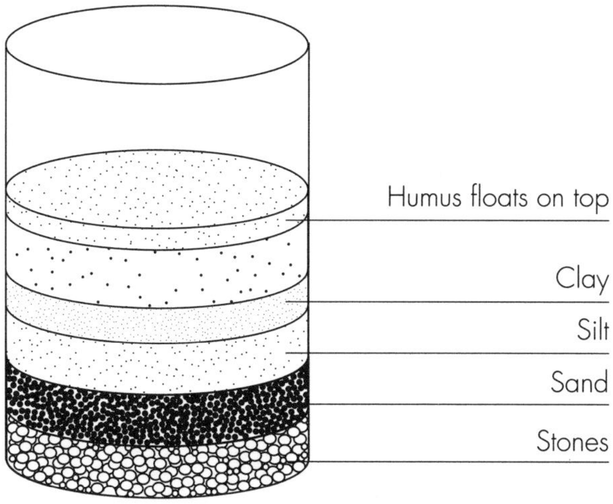

3 Stir well and then leave for a few days to allow the soil to settle into layers.

4 In general, the heavier particles settle to the bottom first.

Activity

Collect some soils from different places and use the settling method described above to compare their contents.

⚠ Warning – cover all cuts before handling soil and wash your hands afterwards.

Soils and plants

Different types of plants grow best on particular soils. For example, rhododendrons and heathers thrive on acid soils, whereas many orchids prefer a limey soil.

Activity

Hydrangeas can be blue, pink or mauve depending on the soil where they grow. Find out what makes the difference. Colour in the flowers and put in the space the word that describes the type of soil for the colour you have chosen.

This hydrangea is growing on ________________ soil.

Building up

Activity

Find some stones from as many different places as possible. Imagine that millions of years ago they were once part of a mountain. Find some clues as to what the rock once looked like.

1 Look for layers. This could mean that the mountain was formed gradually in layers.

2 Try rubbing it with your finger. Does any powder get onto your finger? If so, the layers were probably formed without too much pressure. White or pale grey rock is often limestone – formed from the remains of dead sea-creatures. Red rocks may be sandstone.

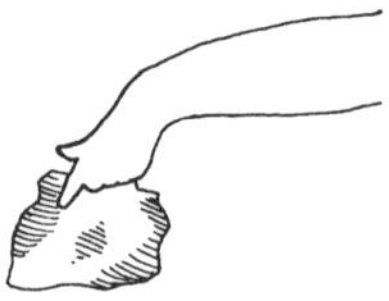

3 Look for crystals. These mean that the rock was probably formed from liquid rock.

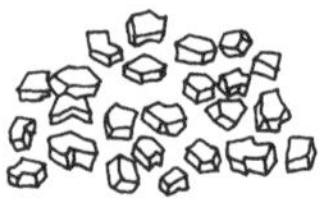

4 Look for one sort of rock inside another. This could have been formed from a hot volcanic explosion (the inner rock) reforming the rock it erupted through (the outer rock).

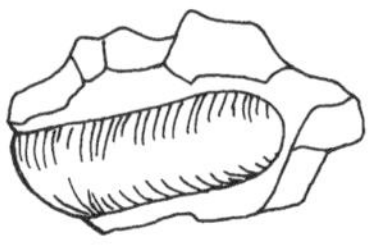

There are three main kinds of rock:

Igneous Rocks formed from volcanoes (eg granite).

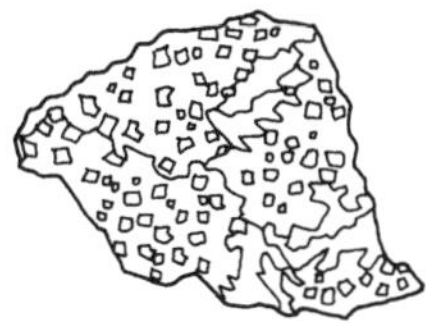

Sedimentary Rocks put down in layers of small particles (eg limestone, mudstone).

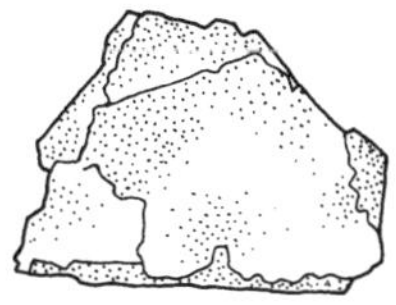

Metamorphic Rocks formed by reforming (changing) igneous or sedimentary rocks (eg marble and slate).

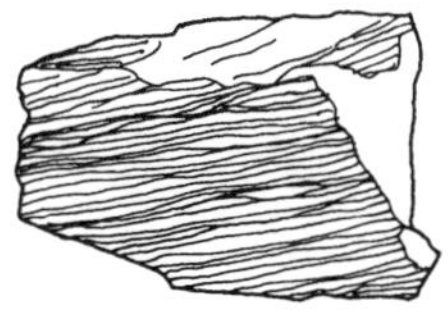

Solids, liquids and gases

Ice is a **solid**, water is a **liquid** and steam is a **gas**. They are all forms of water even though they seem very different. If we think about ice, water and steam, we can find out a lot about the properties of solids, liquids and gases.

An ice cube has a fixed shape
but if we heat it, it melts and loses its shape.

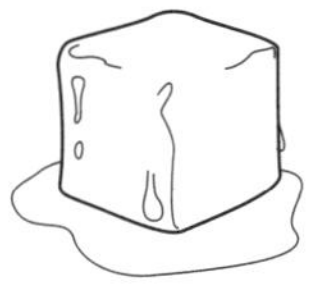

Water has no shape of its own. It will take the shape of the bottom of whatever container it is in. If it is in a cup, it is cup-shaped. If it is in a saucepan, it is pan-shaped and so on.

Steam has even less shape. It will quickly spread to fill the whole of a container, not just the bottom. For example, if you boil water in a saucepan without a lid, the steam will spread through the whole kitchen. Other gases (like air) are the same.

Activity

If you have a freezer or ice box in your refrigerator, here is a challenge for you. Turn a cupful of water into the shape of an animal. You will need some Plasticine or modelling clay to do it.

Imagine being hit on the head by an icicle. Because solids have a fixed shape they often feel hard.

Plasticine is a solid that can feel quite soft. You can change it from one shape to another but you cannot squash it into a smaller space.

Liquids, because they do not have a fixed shape, feel soft – a bucket of water poured over you would make a mess but wouldn't hurt too much.

Liquids do not always seem so soft, as you will know if you have done a 'belly-flop' into a swimming pool.

A breeze in your face will hardly be felt at all, because gases are so soft.

Activity

You will need a plastic syringe for this – such as an icing sugar syringe.

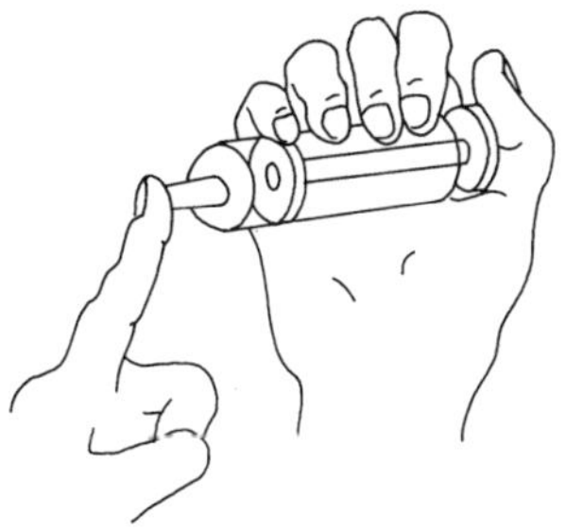

Try squashing the air in the syringe. You should manage to squeeze it into a smaller space.

Do the same with water. You might be surprised to find that you can't squash it at all.

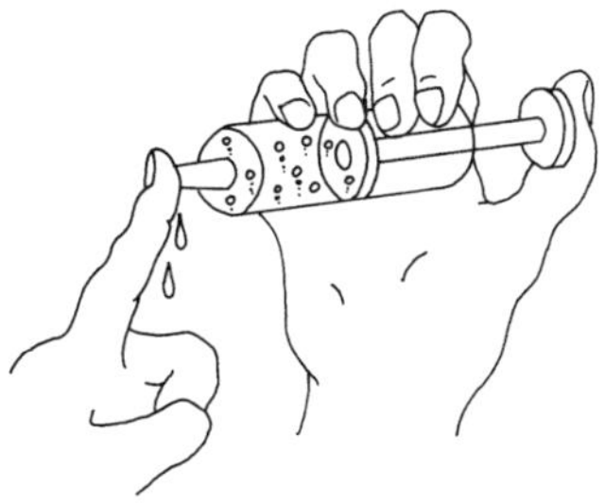

Activity

Fill in the table below to show what gases, liquids and solids are like.

	Solid	Liquid	Gas
Shape		Takes the shape of the bottom of the container	
Do they flow?			Yes
Squashy?	No		

The same amount of material takes up much more space when it is a gas than when it is a liquid or a solid.

Question

If you boiled a kettleful of water completely into steam, how many kettlefuls of steam do you think would you get?

Tick the correct answer.

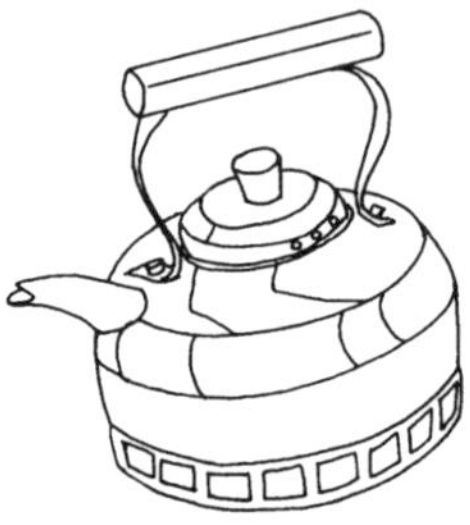

a About 10 ☐
b About 50 ☐
c One ☐
d About 1500 ☐

Often we have to use a gas, a liquid or a solid for a particular job as neither of the others would do.

Questions

1 We couldn't fill a bouncy castle with anything but a gas – imagine one full of a solid! Why would this not be a good idea?

____

____

2 Fuels for cars are most convenient in liquid form. Why is this?

____

____

3 Why are bicycle tyres filled with air, which is a gas? Try to think of two reasons.

____

____

2 Changing materials

Solutions

If you add a spoonful of sugar to a cup of water and stir it well, the sugar seems to completely disappear. But, if you taste the water now you will know the sugar is still there and it still tastes as sweet. The sugar has **dissolved** in the water. You now have a mixture of water and sugar, but the sugar is broken up into such tiny particles that you can't see them. In fact they are so small that they can't be seen under the most powerful microscope. We call this mixture of a solid dissolved in water a **solution**. A solution is always see-through.

Activity

Hold up the following mixtures to the light. Are they solutions?

- Milk ____________________
- Orange squash ____________________
- Lemonade ____________________
- Salty water ____________________

Changing back

We can get the sugar back from our solution by leaving the cup on a windowsill. This time the water will seem to disappear. It has changed from liquid to gas. We call this **evaporation**. It is like very slow boiling.

Activity

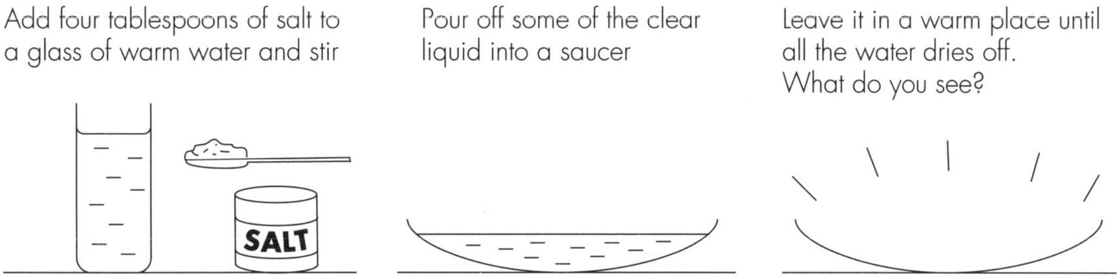

Dissolving salt and leaving it to evaporate

Changes where we can get back to the substances we started with are called **reversible**.

A reversible change

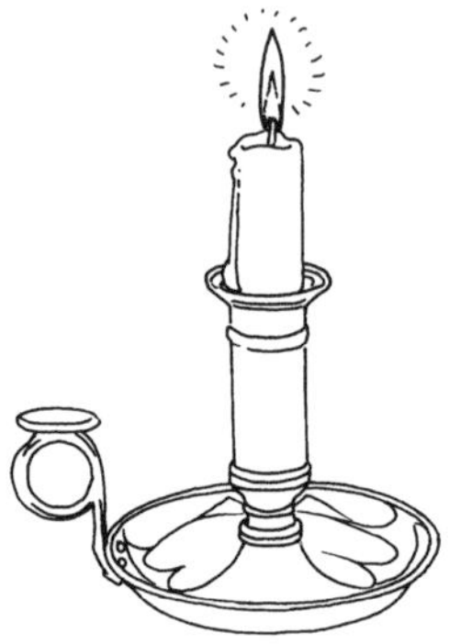

Candle wax is easily turned into a liquid by melting it in a saucepan. It can be cooled to a solid again as a different shaped candle. The wax itself has not changed, only its shape – so this is a reversible change.

Burning a candle is different. This is a change where we cannot get the wax back again.

Activity

Look at the pictures and sort them in the right order for changing a long, thin candle into a short, fat one. Write the numbers in the correct order.

First step Last step

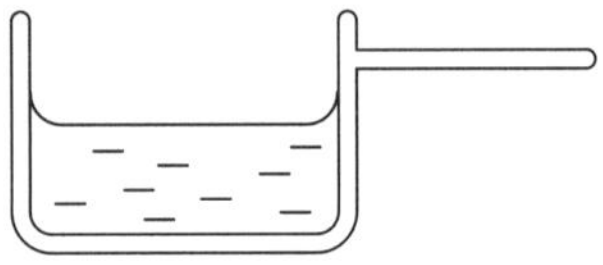

The wax turns to liquid

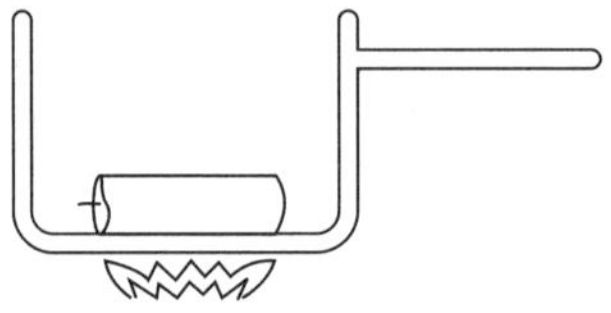

2 *The wax is heated gently in a saucepan*

3 *A long, thin candle made of wax*

The wax cools to make a short, fat candle

5 *The liquid wax is poured into a container*

Don't try this yourself without the help of an adult.

Now, on a separate piece of paper, draw a set of pictures that would turn the short, fat candle into a long, thin one.

As we have seen, heating or cooling a material can often make it change. For example, we can turn water into ice by cooling it and we can turn it into steam by heating it. We can easily undo or reverse these changes. Water, ice and steam are all different forms of the same substance.

Activity

Label the different forms of water in the picture above. Now look at the water cycle on the next page. This only works because water can change forms so easily.

Water cycle

We take water for granted. We have enough water to drink and usually enough to do all sorts of other things. We use it for bathing and showering. Water is used by industry as well as in our homes. Water is a liquid that can be used for so many things. For example:

- it is used in factories for cooling down hot machinery
- it is used in laundries to clean
- it is good at dissolving things and is called the universal **solvent**.

Everything we drink, washing-up liquids, hand creams, ice-creams, shampoos, some paints and varnishes all have water in them.

Activity

On a separate piece of paper, make a list of all the ways you use water at home.

In spite of all these uses, we don't run out of water. This is because water naturally recycles itself.

The important processes involved in the water cycle are evaporation and **condensation**. They have the opposite meaning to each other.

When water evaporates, it changes from water as a liquid to water as an invisible gas. It needs heat to do this. When we hang washing on the line, the water seems to disappear. It evaporates into the air.

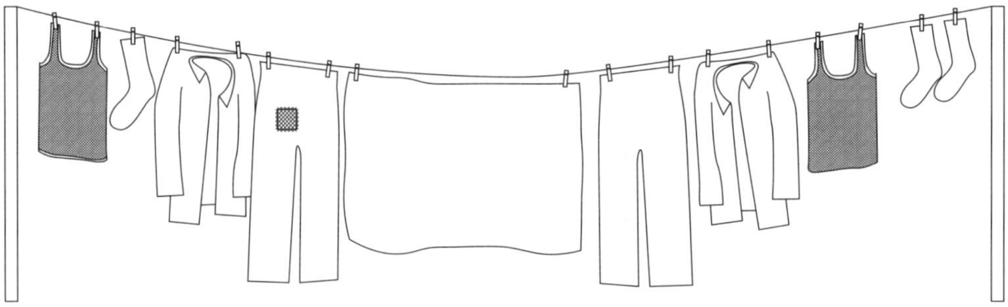

When water condenses it changes from water as a gas in the air to water as a liquid. This happens when it is cool. Water appearing on your windows has condensed because the windows are cooler than the inside of the room.

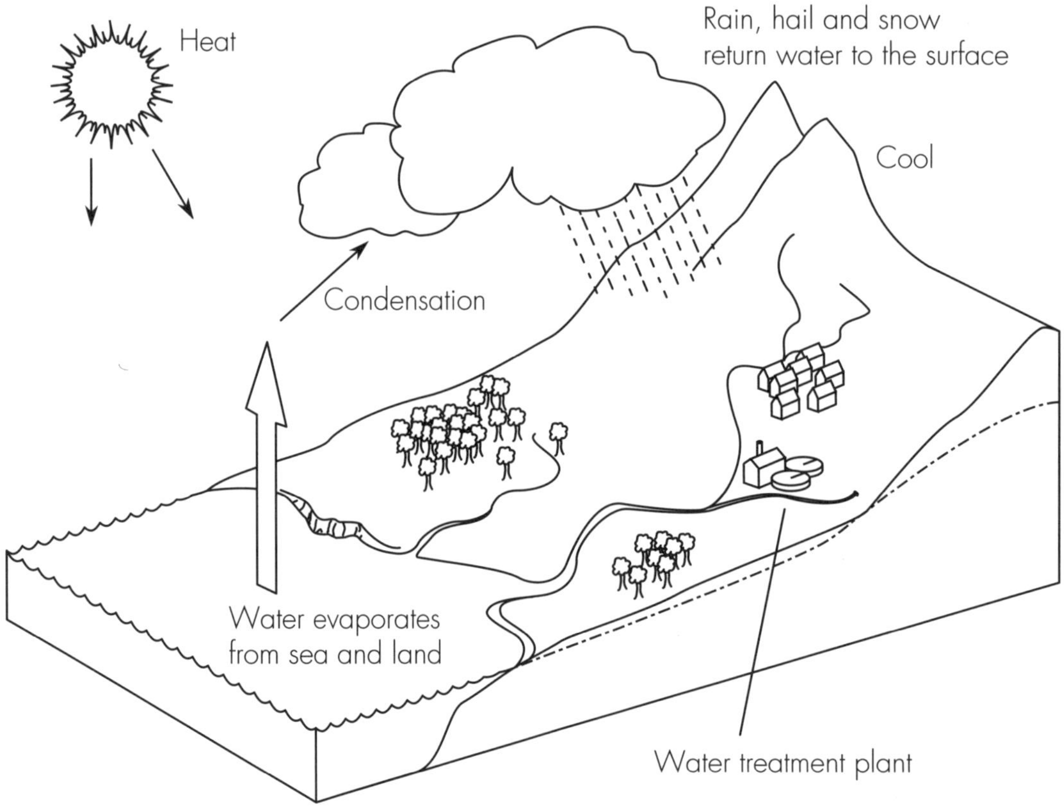

The water cycle

Activity

Colour in the picture of the water cycle on page 22 and then use it to answer the following questions:

1 Where do you think most water evaporates to start the water cycle?

___

2 Where does the heat come from to evaporate the water?

___

3 What makes the water that is in the air as a gas, condense to a liquid and form clouds?

___

___

4 What happens when the drops of water in the clouds get large and heavy?

___

5 How does the water get back to the sea?

___

___

6 What do you think water treatment plants are there for?

___

___

7 In hot countries which have no mountains, the people often have trouble in getting enough water, even though they are next to the sea.

What part of the water cycle is missing in these types of hot countries?

___

___

Activity

Take three cotton handkerchieves or pieces of cotton that are the same size.

Dip each one in water then wring them out so that each one feels about the same wetness. Find a clean surface and do the following:

Spread one handkerchief out flat *Fold one in half* *Fold one into quarters*

Predict which will dry first, second and third and see if you were right. Can you explain why?

Did you know?

Each person in Britain uses an average of 130 litres (30 gallons) of water every day. The biggest single use is flushing the lavatory.

Watering the garden uses about 9 litres (2 gallons) of water every minute.

Industry uses ten thousand million (10 000 000 000) litres of water every day in Britain.

What can you remember?

What do the following words mean?

Evaporation ____________________

Condensation ____________________

Recycling

About a third of our rubbish is made up of metal, glass, paper and packaging. Some of these materials can be **recycled** (used again). This means the materials can be changed back. For example, glass can be melted down. The old glass is used to make new glass. This helps to save **raw materials** and energy.

Activities

1 Why do you think bottle banks have separate bins for different colours of glass?

____

2 What do you think it would be like to live near to a bottle bank?

____

3 Why do you think that you often find bottle banks at big supermarkets?

____

4 Write down what you think happens to a bottle between it being put in the bottle bank and becoming a plate of glass in a window.

____

____

____

____

5 Paper cannot be recycled by melting. Can you explain why?

____

6 Find out which materials other than glass can be recycled by melting.

____

Activity

Start collecting aluminium cans for recycling. You might be able to make some money for your school or a charity.

Changes that cannot be reversed

Some changes cannot be reversed.

When we cook an egg we cannot turn it back into a raw egg, however much we cool it down.

Activity

Tick (✔) the changes below which cannot be easily changed back.

1 Melting some candle wax ☐

2 Making pastry from dough ☐

3 Baking a cake ☐

4 Melting an ice lolly ☐

5 Burning a candle ☐

Do you ever have yogurt for your breakfast or as snack? The picture below shows the steps in making yogurt.

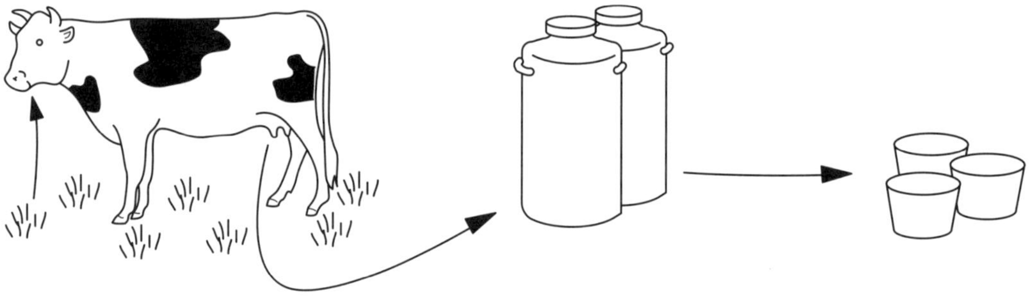

Once we have turned milk into yogurt, we cannot get it back to milk again. The milk has been chemically changed. We say it has been changed by a **chemical reaction** and we have made a new substance.

Activity

Make your own yogurt.

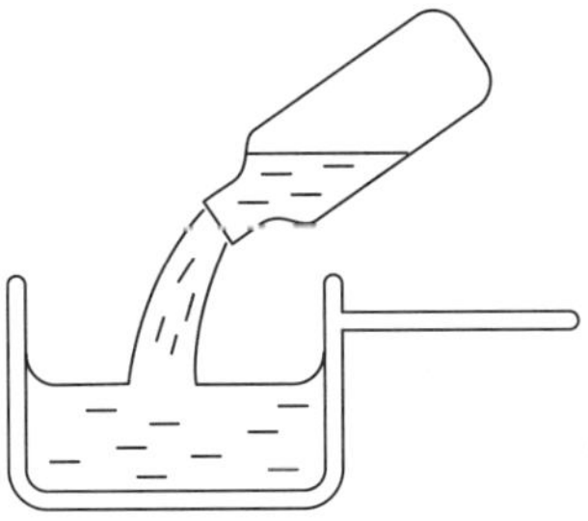

1 Pour a pint of milk into a saucepan.

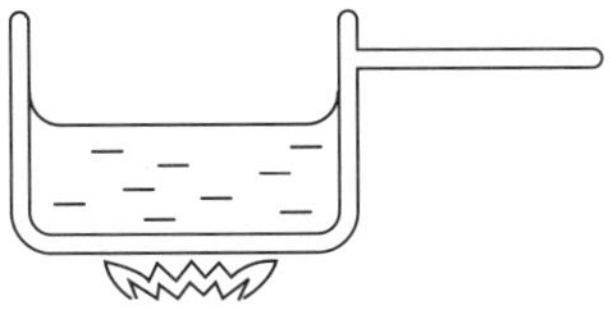

2 Heat gently until it is slightly warm to your (clean) finger.

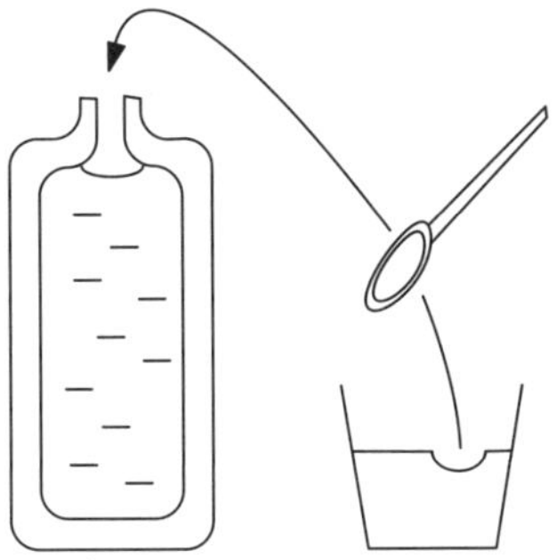

3 Pour into a thermos flask and stir in a tablespoon of live yogurt.

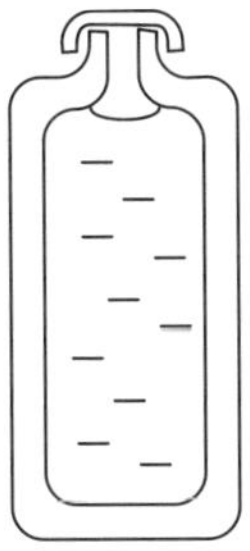

4 Leave for 8 hours.

Make sure that you wash your hands thoroughly and that all containers and equipment are very clean.

Temperature

Have you ever had your temperature taken? If so, you were probably ill enough to feel hot. Your temperature may have been higher than it should be.

Measuring temperature lets us compare how hot or cold things are. Temperature is measured in **degrees celsius** (°C). We use a thermometer to measure temperature.

Activity

Can you read a thermometer?

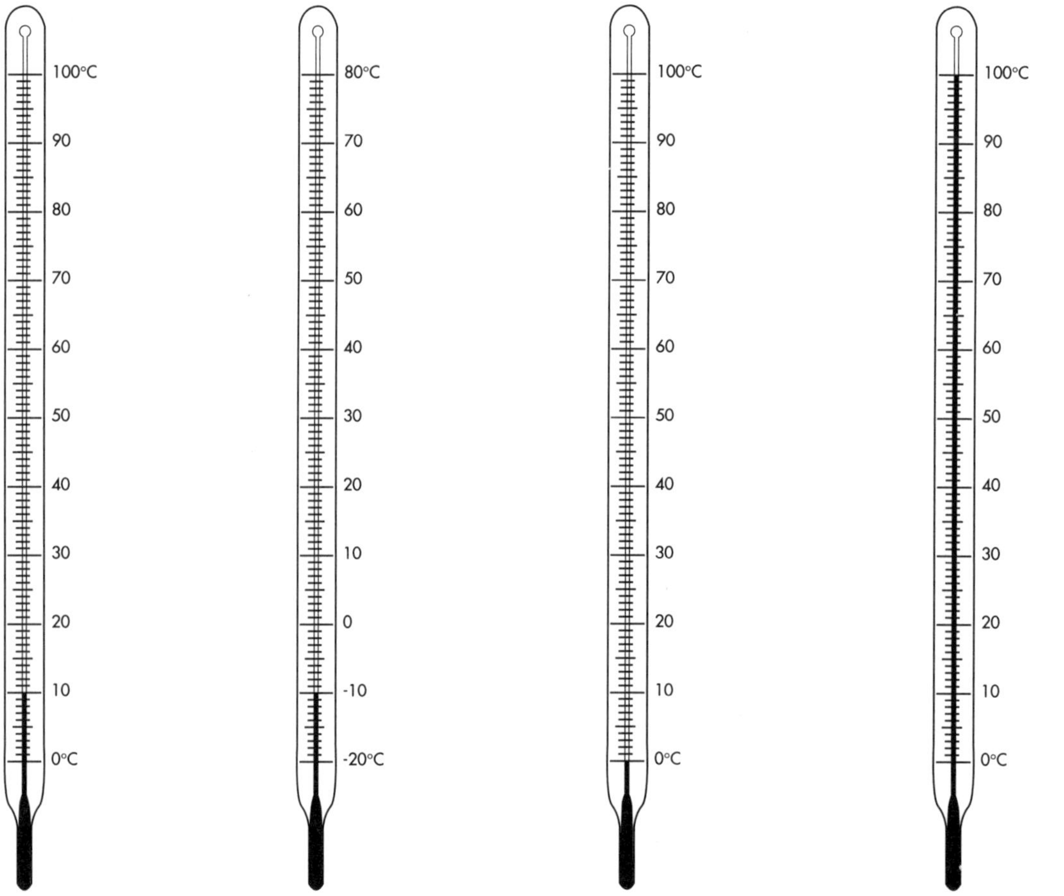

A fridge ____ °C

A freezer ____ °C

An ice cool drink ____ °C

Boiling water ____ °C

Activity

Label the temperatures you have read on the thermometer below. Add any other temperatures you can find.

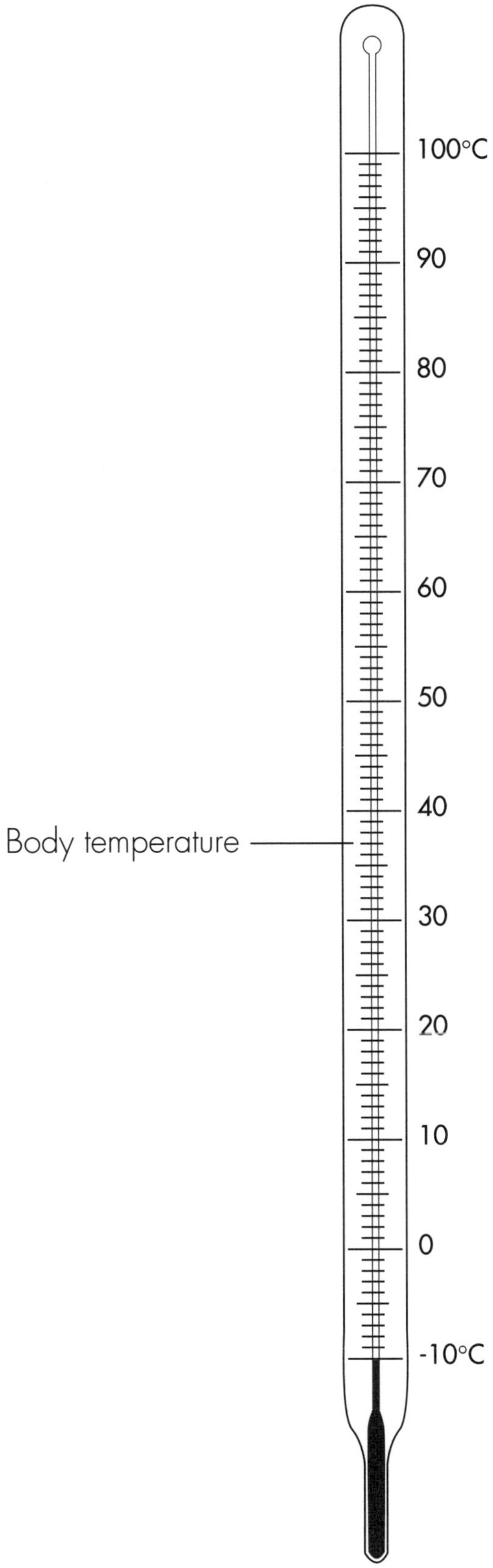

Fuels and burning

Fuels burn and give out heat.

Some people say that when people started using fire it was the first step towards civilisation. It was a way of beating the cold and the dark. The first fuel was probably wood but nowadays we use lots of different fuels.

Activity

Add some more fuels to this list:

wood, coal, petrol ____

____

Fuels use up the oxygen in the air when they burn. Burning is never a reversible change. You can't get the fuel back. So, burning is a chemical reaction and produces waste gases as part of the change. This is not a problem outside with a bonfire, but inside we need to let air into the room and we also need to let the waste gases out.

Activity

Label the diagram below to show where air can get into the room. Where do the waste gases get out?

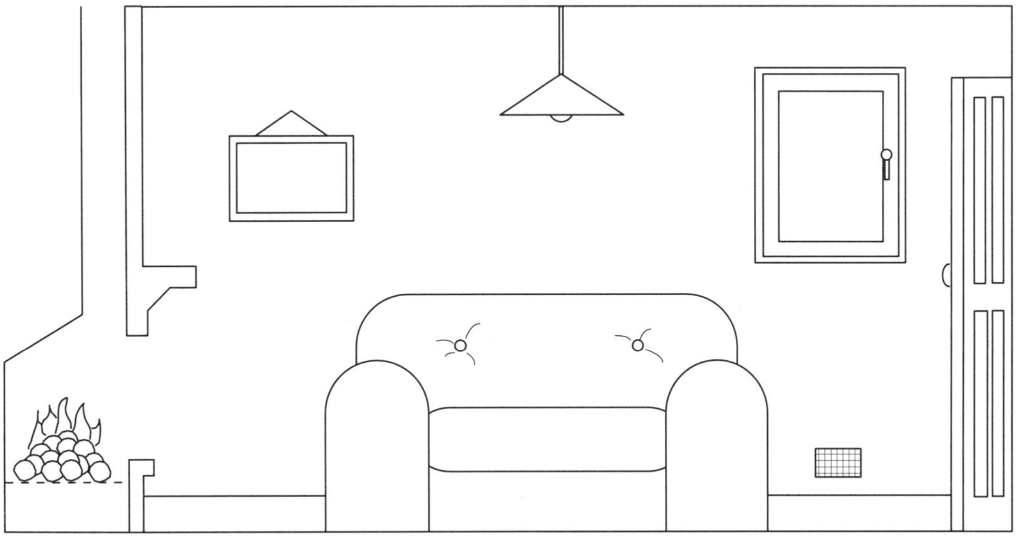

Activity

Set up the following experiment and then answer the questions below.

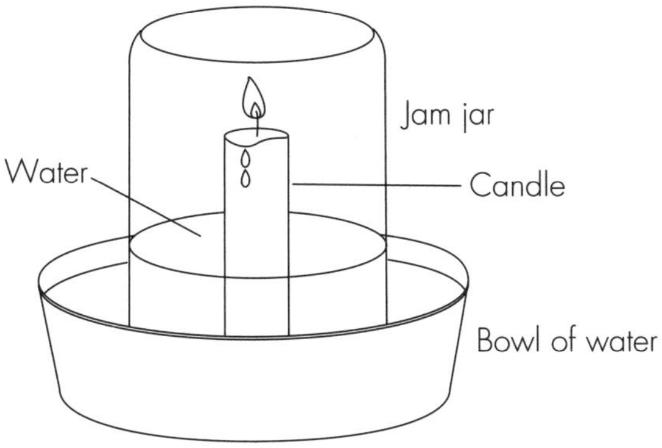

Burning a candle under a jam jar

Take care with matches. Ask an adult to help you.

1 The fuel in the candle is wax. Why do you think it goes out?

____

____

2 Does any of the air seem to be used up? How can you tell?

____

____

The products of burning

Most fuels contain carbon. The black stuff on burnt toast is carbon. When fuels burn, they use oxygen to make an invisible gas called **carbon dioxide**.

When humans burn millions of tonnes of fuel in power stations, homes and factories, the carbon dioxide gas goes into the air around us. Carbon dioxide forms a blanket around the Earth which lets in light from the Sun but stops heat getting out. So the Earth is slowly getting hotter. This is called the **greenhouse effect**.

Fuels also contain hydrogen and this burns to form water. This is why you may see drips of water coming from a car's exhaust pipe on a cold morning.

Did you know?

- Diamond is a very pure form of carbon. The famous French scientist Antoine Lavoisier bought a diamond so that he could burn it to see if it made carbon dioxide.
- The 'lead' used in pencils is actually made from graphite which is another form of carbon.

A new word: the word **combustion** means just the same as **burning**.

What can you remember?

What do the following words mean?

Fuel ____

Combustion or burning ______________________________

Another change that cannot be reversed

Have you ever heard the saying "it's like painting the Forth Bridge"? It means that the task never ends because the bridge is so long. Painters start painting at one end of the bridge and as soon as they reach the other end they need to go back and start again because it is so long.

The Forth Bridge is made of iron. But why do iron bridges need painting at all?

The Forth Bridge

The answer is to stop them **rusting**. Rusting is a chemical change that can happen to iron and steel (which is mostly made of iron) when it is left unprotected in the damp air. The iron changes into a red powdery substance called rust. Iron is a strong metal but rust is weak and flakes away. So a rusting bridge is weaker than it should be and is also slowly disappearing. Rusting can be a very expensive problem.

Did you know?

Steel is iron with small amounts of other substances (such as carbon) added to make it stronger.

Activity

Make a list of any three objects that we try to keep from rusting. Write down how we achieve this for each one. An example has been done for you.

Car bumper plated with chromium (chromium-plated)

____

____

____

Activity

You will need some nails and four screw-topped glass jars such as coffee jars. Clean the nails with sandpaper so that they aren't rusty to start with. Set up the jars as shown below and look at them every day for a couple of weeks. Write down in the table what the nails look like.

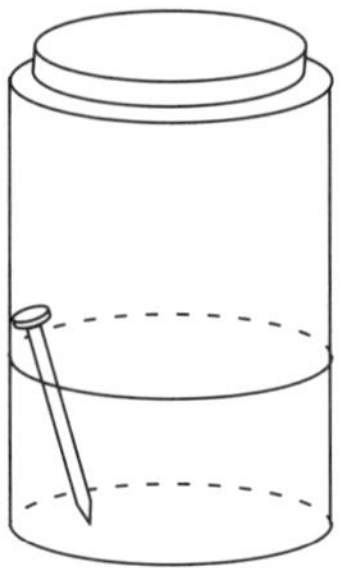

Nail, water and air

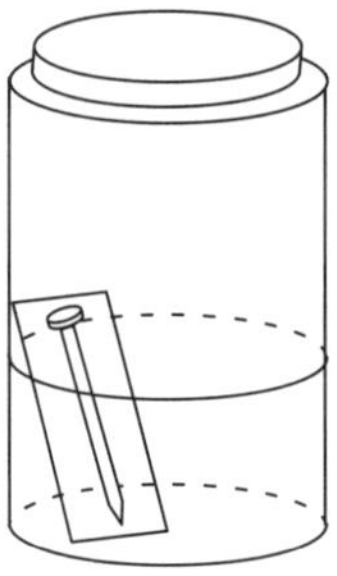

Nail wrapped in sticky tape, water and air

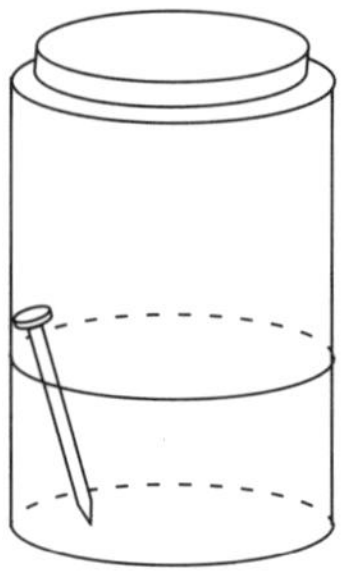

Nail, salty water and air

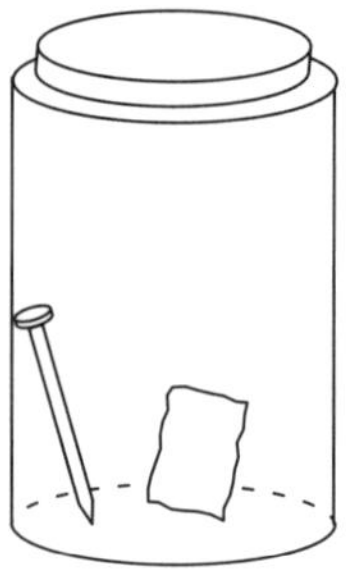

Nail, silica gel and air

Day	Content of jars			
	Nail, water and air	Nail wrapped in sticky tape, water and air	Nail, salty water and air	Nail, silica gel and air

Silica gel soaks up moisture so that the air is really dry. Air will not be able to get at the nail wrapped in sticky tape.

You often find a sachet of silica gel packed with binoculars or electronic equipment to keep them dry.

3 Separating mixtures of materials

Sorting out a mess!

Does your room look like Jack's? The only way Jack can sort out his room is to pick out all the clothes and put them in the cupboard, pick out the books and so on.

Some **mixtures** are more easily separated.

Activity

Show how you might separate the following by drawing arrows between the 'separators' and the mixtures:

'Separators'	Mixtures	
		*Marbles and wooden blocks*
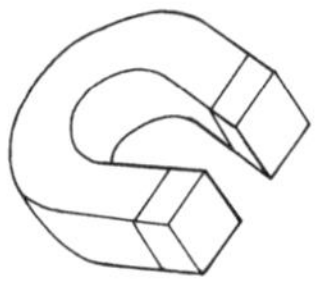	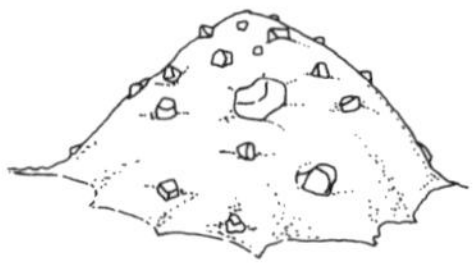	*Pebbles in sand*
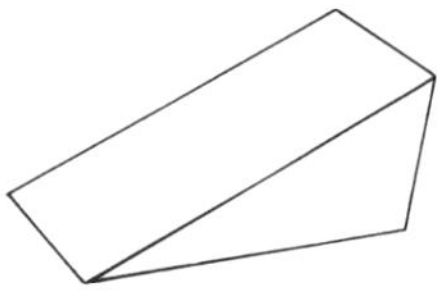	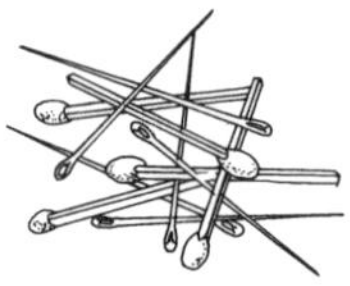	*Needles and matchsticks*

You separated these mixtures by finding a way in which the parts, or **components**, of the mixture were different. We say they have different properties.

Sometimes it is very important that we 'unmix' things.

Sea water is a mixture of water and salt (a solution). We do not drink it, even if we are very thirsty, because it is so salty that it makes us sick.

If we can separate the water from the salt, we have a liquid that we can drink. Separating a mixture lets us find out what each of the substances in the mixture is like on its own. Then we can find out whether they are useful to us. Sea water could be useful to the thirsty sailor in the picture above when separated into water and salt!

Question

Do you think the salt separated from sea water is of any use?

____

____

Activity

Which one of the following ways might get the water separated from salt? Explain how it would work.

Activity

You will need some matchsticks, some metal paper-clips, some 5p pieces, a magnet and a bowl of water.

Put the matchsticks, paper-clips and 5p pieces in a box and shake them up. You have now got a mixture of all three. It could take a long time to sort them out again, but not if you are clever.

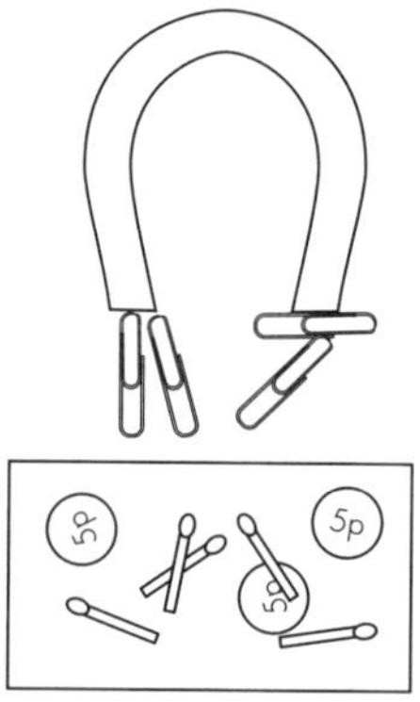

Stick the magnet into the mixture. This will pull out all the paper-clips.

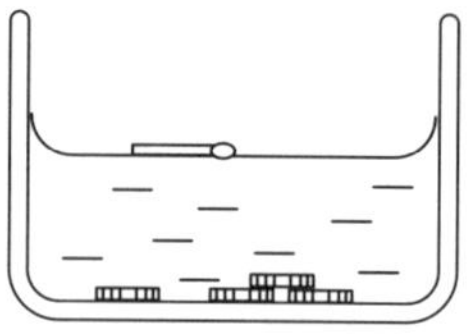

Now pour the matchsticks and 5p pieces into the bowl of water. The matchsticks will float and the coins will sink. You've done it!

Which properties allow you to separate the different things from the mixture? Complete the table with the words which describe these properties

	First separation	Second separation
Paper-clips	are..........................	____________
5p pieces	are not.....................	.....................in water
Matchsticks	are not.....................	.....................in water

1 Why wouldn't this method work to separate a mixture of paper-clips, drawing-pins and 5p pieces?

____

2 How could you separate a mixture of salt and rice? Hint – something in the kitchen might help.

____

3 What properties of salt and rice let you separate them?

____

Activity

Challenge your friends or parents! Think up a mixture of two or more everyday things and see if they can work out a way of separating them. Beware! You lose the game if you can't do it yourself!

Separating by sieving

We can use sieves of different sizes to trap the larger particles in a mixture.

Activity

Look at the mixtures below and the different sieves. Match the mixture with the sieve which will work best and fastest.

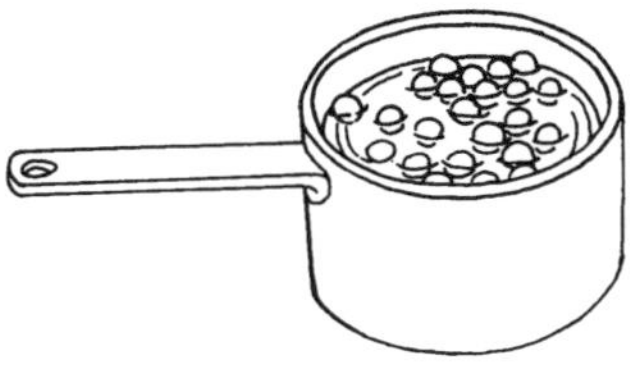

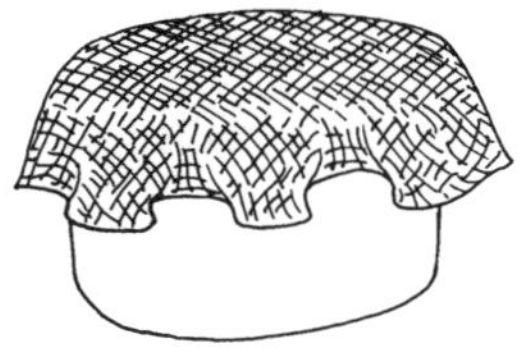

Peas in water

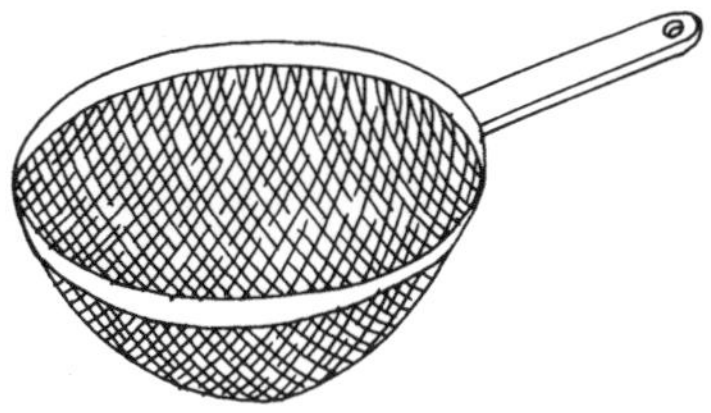

Lumps in flour

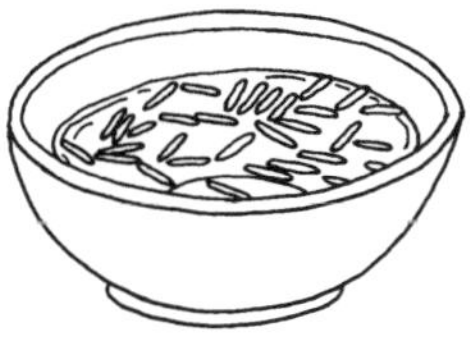

Rice in water

Soil sieves

Dry soils can be separated by using a set of sieves with smaller and smaller holes.

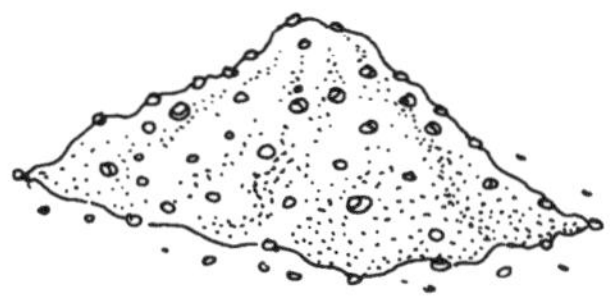

Filtering

We can use paper as a sieve and we call this **filtering**. We need paper when the particles we are trying to stop are very small.

Question

Why do we use a tea-strainer for tea leaves, but filter paper for filtering ground coffee?

___

___

This doesn't work with solids that dissolve in water. You couldn't filter the salt from a salt solution. If you filter salt water it still tastes salty.

Activity

Make the following mixtures and then try to separate them again by filtering. You will need either filter paper or filters for coffee. A funnel to put the paper in will make it easier.

a 1 teaspoon of crushed chalk in a cup of water.

b 1 teaspoon of sand in a cup of water.

c 1 teaspoon of sodium bicarbonate in a cup of water.

d 1 teaspoon of sugar in a cup of water.

Questions

1 Which two of these mixtures formed a solution?

___

2 Why does filtering not work with a solution?

___

Ink blots

Did you know that many inks are mixtures of different dyes?

There is a special way to separate these dyes. You will need some blotting paper and a cup or glass plus some water-soluble felt-tipped pens.

Activity

1 Cut out a circle of blotting paper and, using a felt-tipped pen, put a small dot in the middle.

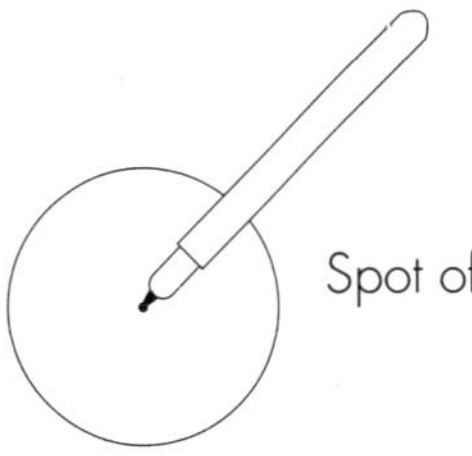

2 Place the circle on a glass and drop a spot of water onto the ink dot.

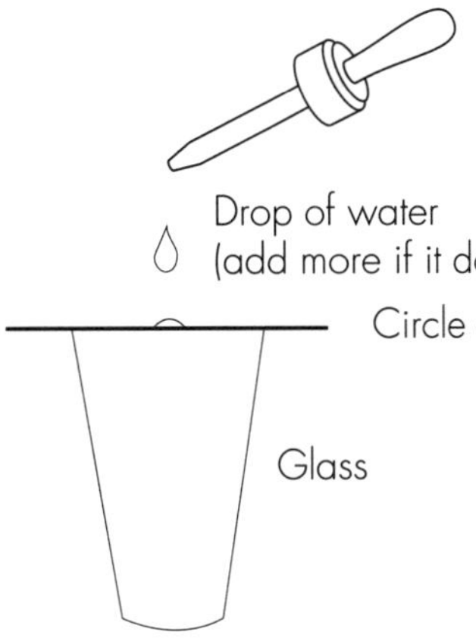

3 The ink will gradually spread out and any different colours will separate out.

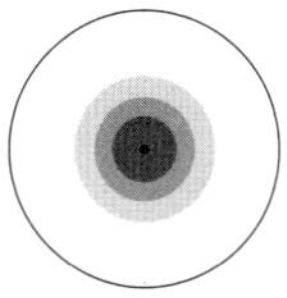

How does it work?

As the ink spreads, imagine a tug-of-war between the blotting paper and the water. The paper tries to hold the dye where it is and the water tries to pull it away. Each dye in the ink is different so each spreads at a different rate.

Activity

Make a table of the different colours in your felt-tipped pens. Find another brand of the same colour and see if the dyes are the same.

	Colour of pen	Colours present
1		
2		
3		
4		
5		
6		

Why would this not work for pens that were not water-soluble?

Another way of separating the dyes is to use a strip of blotting paper instead of a circle. The water spreads up the blotting paper.

Activity

Find out if this is a better method of separating the colours.

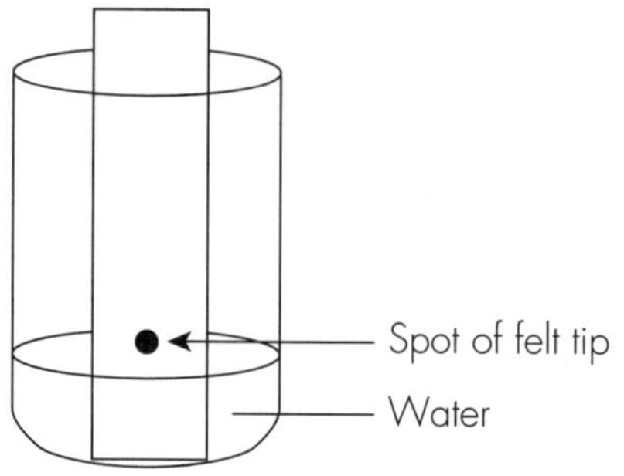

More about solutions

When a solid dissolves in a liquid we have a solution. The liquid is usually water, though it needn't be. When so much solid is added so that no more will dissolve then we have a **saturated solution**.

Different solids dissolve to a different extent so that different saturated solutions will have different amounts of solids in them.

Activity

Half fill two glasses with water. They need to be the same size to make this a fair test.

To glass A add ½ teaspoon of salt and stir until it disappears (ie the salt has dissolved). Add more ½ teaspoons while stirring, counting the number you put in. Go on doing this until no more salt dissolves.

To glass B do the same thing, but using ½ teaspoons of sugar.

1 Which solid dissolved most?

____

____

2 Find out if hot water makes a difference to your answer. Write about your results.

____

____

Word list

Burning	This is when a fuel combines with oxygen in the air and gives out heat and flames
Carbon dioxide	This is a gas formed when fuels are burned (and by breathing)
Chemical reaction	This is when one substance changes into a different one. The change is usually hard to reverse
Combustion	Another word for burning (see above)
Component	One of the parts of a mixture
Condensation	The process of a gas turning into a liquid. For example, water vapour turning into water as it cools
Conduct	Allow something to flow through (eg heat or electricity)
Degrees celsius	Units of measurement used for temperature
Dissolve	If a solid is added to a liquid and it disappears, we say it dissolves
Electrical conductor	A material which lets electricity flow through it
Electrical insulator	A material which does not let electricity flow through it
Erosion	The grinding down of small pieces of rock (such as pebbles) into smaller bits (such as sand)
Evaporation	The process of liquid turning to gas. For example, liquid water turning into water vapour
Filtering	The process of separating solids by sieving (usually through mesh or paper)
Fuel	A substance which can burn and give out energy
Gas	A substance which has no shape of its own and completely fills the whole of its container
Greenhouse effect	The warming of our atmosphere by the presence of gases like carbon dioxide which trap heat
Humus	The part of soil formed by the breakdown of living material, eg dead leaves, plants and animals
Igneous rock	Rock that is formed by cooling liquid rock
Insulator	A **heat** insulator is a material which does not allow heat to flow through it An **electrical** insulator is a material which does not allow electricity to flow through it

Liquid	A substance which has no shape of its own and fills the bottom of its container only
Materials	Substances which have their own particular properties
Metamorphic rock	Rock that has been formed from other rocks being changed by heat and pressure
Mixture	A mixture contains two or more different substances. These can usually be separated fairly easily
Property	This describes what a material is like in itself. All samples of the material will have the same properties. Examples include 'magnetic' or 'transparent' or 'red'
Raw material	A natural material which is used as the starting point for making some new material
Recycle	Use materials again often by melting them down and re-moulding them
Reversible	A reversible change is one that can easily be undone
Rusting	The eating away of iron and steel when it is exposed to air and water
Saturated solution	A solution in which no more solid will dissolve
Sedimentary rock	Rock formed by layers of particles
Solid	A material that has, and can keep, a definite shape
Solution	A mixture of a solid and a liquid which you can see through
Solvent	A liquid which will dissolve a solid
Substance	Something with its own particular properties

Answers

Note: There is more than one correct answer to many of the questions. Not all have answers – some provide a basis for further discussion.

Pages 3-4

1 Pillar box – red.
2 Plate – it is the only one not made of metal.
3a Same shape: brick, TV and butter.
b Not hard when you touch them: cushion, butter.
c Alone: cup.
d In both sets: butter.
e Yellow flower: buttercup.

Page 5

1 Waterproof: rubber, PVC, etc.
2 Flexible (bendy): Rubber, etc.
3 All liquids have the property of being runny.
4 All perfumes have the property of being smelly.

Jug, spectacles and window pane are all made of glass. The property that is important is transparency.

Better to have discovered iron rather than gold as it is stronger and more useful for making things.

Page 6

Newspaper gets wet. It will tear, etc.

A rubber hammer is flexible and not rigid enough to push a nail in.

Page 7

1 Wigwam = skins or leather.
Igloo = snow or ice.
Hut = wood.
2 Wigwam is best for moving around as can easily be folded up and carried.
4 Igloo is most uncomfortable as probably cold.

Page 8

Window	Glass because it is transparent.
Roof tiles	Slate because it is hard-wearing and strong.
Door	Wood because it can be painted
Gutter	Plastic because it is easy to mould into shape and is waterproof.
Door handle	Brass because it is shiny and nice to look at.

Page 9

Any sensible answer. Possible test: Put hot water in a tin can with thermometer. Wrap can with one glove, and record temperature at intervals. Repeat with other gloves, keeping other factors constant.

Polar bears are covered in fur.
Seals are covered in thick skin and fatty layers.
Birds have feathers.
Surfers wear wetsuits.

Page 10

a Oven glove to prevent getting burnt, made from thick material which does not conduct heat.
b Teapot needs to be a good insulator to keep the tea warm. Made from china or other pottery.
c Lagged immersion heater needs to be a good insulator to keep water warm. Lagging made from thick material which traps air, eg foamed plastic.

Page 11 Handle and handle on lid of kettle are made of heat insulators to prevent us burning our hands.

Page 12 Sand drained most quickly because the soil particles are larger than the other two samples, hence the water drains more easily.

Page 17

	Solid	Liquid	Gas
Shape	Retains its own shape	Takes the shape of the bottom of the container	Takes the shape of the whole container
Do they flow?	No	Yes	Yes
Squashy?	No	No	Yes

Page 18 Correct answer: d About 1500

1 A bouncy castle filled with a solid would not be bouncy!
2 Fuel in liquid form is easier to use for filling a fuel tank as it flows but does not escape.
3 Bicycle tyres are filled with air because it is squashy and easy to pump in to tyres by using a hand pump.

Page 19 Milk is not a solution.
Orange squash is not a solution.
Lemonade is a solution.
Salty water is a solution.

Page 20 Correct order: 3, 2, 1, 5, 4.

Page 21 The different forms of water in the picture are: ice (snow), water (rain). The cloud contains water as tiny droplets.

Page 23

1 Water evaporates most from the sea.
2 Heat comes from the Sun to evaporate the water.
3 The water in air condenses to form clouds as it cools down over the mountains.
4 When clouds get large and heavy it rains.
5 Water gets back to the sea via rivers and streams.
6 Water treatment plants purify water and make it safe to drink.
7 The cooling part of the water cycle is missing (ie mountains).

Page 24 The handkerchief which is spread out flat will dry out first because it has the greatest surface area exposed from which the water can evaporate. The hankie which is folded most will dry out last as it has the least surface area exposed.

For definitions of evaporation and condensation, see the *Word list* on pages 44 and 45.

Page 25

1 The colour cannot be removed.
2 Convenient, may be noisy at times.
3 Convenient for shoppers, central point, used by lots of people.
4 Bottle to bank; factory where washed and melted down; then remoulded.
5 It will burn, not melt.
6 Many metals, some plastics.

You may like to contact: The Aluminium Can Recycling Centre, I-Mex House, 52 Blucher Street, Birmingham B1 1QU.

Page 26 Easily changed back:

1 Melting some candle wax.
4 Melting an ice lolly.

Page 28 Temperatures: fridge 10°C, freezer -10°C, ice cool drink 0°C, boiling water 100°C.

Page 30 Other fuels include: oil, coke, alcohol, gas.

Page 31 Air gets in through the window, door and airbricks. Waste gases escape up the chimney.

1 The candle goes out because there is no longer enough oxygen for burning.
2 Some of the air has been used up as the water has risen up the jar.

Page 33 For definitions of fuel and combustion or burning, see the *Word list* on pages 44 and 45.

Page 34 Examples of rusting and its prevention: bicycle gears – oil or grease; car bodies – paint; (some) nails – zinc plating.

Page 36 Use the sieve to separate pebbles from sand. Use a magnet to separate the needles from the matchsticks and use the slope to separate marbles from the wooden blocks.

Page 37 Salt separated from sea water can be used for food preservation or for treating icy roads.

The saucepan with the lid partly off. Some pure water condenses on the lid and drips off leaving the salt in the pan.

Page 38

	First separation	Second separation
Paper-clips	are.........magnetic...	———————
5p pieces	are not....magnetic...	........sink.......in water
Matchsticks	are not....magnetic...	........float.....in water

1 Both drawing-pins and paper-clips are magnetic.
2 Sieve, to separate salt and rice; or dissolve the salt in water.
3 Salt will go through a sieve and rice will not; or salt will dissolve in water, rice will not.

Page 39 Separate the peas from the water by using a colander; lumps from the flour by using a fine sieve; and rice from water by using a piece of muslin (the last two could be the other way round).

Page 40 Tea leaves are larger than coffee grains so we use a tea strainer. Filter paper is required to filter coffee as it contains fine particles.

1 Sodium bicarbonate and sugar both form solutions when dissolved in water.
2 Filtering does not work because particles have dissolved into a solution.

Page 42 This method depends on the ink being water-soluble and would therefore not work if the pens were not water-soluble.

St And[illegible] Church, Fortrose Ross-shire

Text: Elizabeth Sutherland
Layout, Photographs: Elizabeth Waters and Hayden Jeffrey, Kevin Swanson

Helen
Love & Blessings
Elizabeth Sutherland

Printed and Published by For The Right Reasons
16th April 2017

ISBN 978-1-910205-97-6

Dedication

To all members of St Andrew of Scotland's Church, past and present, priests, office-bearers and congregations who have beautified St Andrews with their presence and their prayers.

Acknowledgements

This fourth short history of St Andrews Scottish Episcopal Church, Fortrose, owes much to the research and scholarship to be found in previous booklets, now sadly out of print. The first, entitled **The Banner of St Boniface,** was written anonymously and printed in 1929 to commemorate the twentieth anniversary of the Consecration.

The second booklet entitled **A Brief Account of St Andrews Episcopal Church** written by Louise B. Turner was printed in 1982. Lady Turner, a scholar, lived in Cathedral Square and her booklet was carefully researched from the old records.

In 2000 Colonel Angus Fairrie, a historian, edited Lady Turner's booklet and brought it up to date. This too is out of print as is my own account of **Canon Spence Ross: His Life and Legacy** published in 2008.

This edition commemorates the 190th birthday of the original and incomplete church which was opened for worship on November 1st, All Saints Day, 1827.

My thanks to Elizabeth Waters for her artistic design and splendid illustrations and Hayden Jeffrey for photographs, to Canon Mel Langille and Ramsay McGhee for advice, information and encouragement. ES

Foreword

Come to him, a living stone,
though rejected by mortals
and like living stones, let yourselves be built into a spiritual house,
to be a holy priesthood,
to offer spiritual sacrifices acceptable to God
through Jesus Christ.

1 Peter 2 v 4-5

Saint Andrew of Scotland is a truly wonderful church with an amazing history. The building that houses that church is equally beautiful and historic. Built not long after it became possible for Episcopalians, after the long years of penal prohibition, to worship in the open, it is truly a gem.

Generations of faithful lay people and fine priests have worshipped within her hallowed walls, offering the Eucharistic Sacrifice to God's glory and being fed in order to lovingly reach out and extend Christ's Kingdom of justice, love and peace.

To say I am humbled to be writing a Foreword for a book by Elizabeth does not come close to describing how I feel. There is no one more qualified to bring Saint Andrew's history to life! Whether you are part of the Saint Andrew's family or not, let her draw you into the history and, all too soon, you'll know you are welcome, cherished and drawn into the warm embrace of a church worthy of the name.

Canon Mel Langille
Rector
St Boniface
(Curadan)
March 2017

Welcome to St Andrews Scottish Episcopal Church!

All churches are special places. This is certainly true of St Andrews for three very good reasons. Firstly, because it was built, preserved and beautified by generous hands, hopeful hearts and loving souls to the glory of God. Secondly, because it represents both change and continuity rising from the ruins of its neighbour, Ross's thirteenth century cathedral, in an often turbulent, sometimes meandering, but never stagnant river of worship. Thirdly, because it is a consecrated place, set apart from the world yet in it, hallowed by the prayers of generations and sanctified by the presence of Jesus Christ in the Reserved Sacrament of which we are reminded by the lighted lamp that hangs in the sanctuary.

Coull's Chapel

St Andrews was by no means the first Episcopal place of worship in Fortrose as is evidenced by Bishop Robert Forbes who in his Journal described how in 1770 he found there *a handsome chapel and a crowded audience* where he confirmed 259 souls. This chapel in Academy Street had been built by Alexander Mackenzie of Coull to replace the meeting-house burned down during the fractious Jacobite era when Episcopalianism was proscribed by the Hanoverian government for its loyalty to the Stuart monarchy. Once known as Coull's Chapel, the building was rescued and restored in 1897 and became St Andrews Church Hall. However, the fabric of the building is once again in urgent need of repair and options for its restoration are being considered by the Vestry.

It now houses a thriving charity shop.

The Original St Andrews Church

St Andrews Church was planned as early as 1790 when Hector Mackenzie of Flowerburn granted the feu of the land on the Braehead stipulating that a church of the value of at least *£1,200 be built thereon, and no other building*. (A useful stipulation when some century later the Town Council proposed building public toilets alongside the church!)

The Inverness Journal recorded that *the new Episcopal Chapel at Fortrose was opened on the 1st November 1827 in the presence of several clergymen and a respectable and crowded congregation. After the usual service and an excellent and appropriate sermon...a collection was made in the aid of the funds which are still deficient nearly £300. The elegant edifice, which was built by subscription is of pure Gothic architecture and stands overlooking the Moray Firth and is conspicuously seen from Inverness, Fort George and the surrounding country. The deficiency of its funds, it is hoped, may still be made up by further contributions from the well-disposed...The pews for the poorer classes are rent-free and the service is performed in English and Gaelic under the superintendence of the Bishop of Ross and Argyll.*

The Statistical Account of 1843 repeats the description of St Andrews as a *handsome Gothic building far in advance of its time.*

Although open for worship and served by itinerant priests or lay-readers mainly from St Johns, Arpafeelie, the church could not be consecrated for it was still in debt. Nor was it universally admired. The Revd John Mason Neale in *Ecclesiastical Notes* of 1848 described it as *a horrible conglomeration of pinnacles without chancel, without any one good point.*

From the earliest surviving plan of the building dating from 1890 it appears to have been a plain rectangular building with buttresses at the west end. The two at the east end are not delineated but the bonding suggests that they are original and the north- east buttress is actually within the vestry (added in 1913).

Although no detailed description of the interior has come to light, we know that it was built of ashlar box with Georgian plastered walls panelled in wood for about half way up its walls. This is known because in 1911 the walls had to be stripped of their panelling and burned because of dry rot which had spread to part of the floor and the pews.

The main entrance was through the west gable. Part of the back of the church was curtained off to provide a robing room for the choir and a vestry on either side of the aisle. At the east end there was an 'American organ' on loan from the Fletchers of Rosehaugh, an altar in the centre and a pulpit on the south side which was probably no more than a lectern on a podium while the font was a pewter basin on a stand.

In 1851 the Right Revd Robert Eden, Bishop of Moray, Ross and Caithness, an aristocratic Tractarian, devoted follower of the Oxford Movement and an Englishman of authority, substance and evangelical zeal was consecrated. It was he who recognised the young Aberdeenshire schoolmaster, John Ramsay Spence Ross's potential, and inspired him to bring his wife Ruth and their three small children to the village of Avoch where he was appointed both as schoolmaster to the Episcopal school (the Mackenzie Foundation) and lay reader at Fortrose and Cromarty chapels.

The Revd John Ramsay Spence Ross (later Canon of Inverness Cathedral)

Spence Ross (as he was always known) came to Avoch in 1879 and three years later was ordained a priest and the first rector of St Andrews. He continued, however, to live in the schoolmaster's house in Avoch and to administer both school and parish. Ironic this for the teacher, latterly a Mr Brayshaw, lived in Fortrose and walked everyday to Avoch!

Spence Ross was a man of many talents. His singing voice, such an asset in a clergyman, was outstanding. He was much in demand socially for his ability to tell humorous stories in a broad Buchan accent. He genuinely loved children, he curled, he gardened knowledgeably, was fascinated by archaeology and a founder member and Past Master of the Seaforth Masonic Lodge in Fortrose. He also enjoyed a dram. One probably apochryphal tale tells of a dinner party at Meadowbank where his host Major-General MacIntyre produced a fine whisky. Later he was assisted into his pony cart and the pony, needing no guidance, trotted him, blissfully unaware, home safely to Avoch.

A New St Andrews

Above all Spence Ross was an enthusiast and a visionary. He, and from 1886 the newly consecrated Bishop James B.K. Kelly, wanted St Andrews to be no longer a dependent mission chapel but an independent church in the new catholic tradition with its own Rector, Constitution and Board of Managers (Vestry). For this to happen many improvements were needed.

In 1888 he gathered his congregation together in the Royal Hotel to discuss the future. The Church had never been debt free, thus never consecrated, the fabric was already deteriorating and Spence Ross's stipend £75 per annum. A massive fund-raising programme was proposed. Contributions came in from all over Britain many as little as a shilling, a few as much as five pounds, the result of a series of bazaars and concerts, shadow pantomimes and *tableaux vivants.* Between 1891 and 1904 including loans and grants from central church funds, the amount raised came to £631 19/7d.

On November 27 1891, the Board of Managers met again. A Constitution was agreed and the first Minutes kept with Spence Ross himself as Treasurer and Chairman. Work defined as *a suitable Heating Apparatus* was agreed. *Messrs Ross and Macbeth were chosen as architects* and *the Rector was granted permission to make* ***certain specified alterations at the east end of the Church****, he* [Spence Ross] *understanding to find money to meet the expenditure with such alterations as this would necessitate.*

These '*certain alterations'* included a chancel, vestry and organ chamber at the east end of the church. Fundraising continued and the architect contacted. A Baptistry is not mentioned.

Considering all that followed, the responsibility, the building and the stress of on-going and intense fundraising, this was a monumental decision.

Alexander Ross, Architect

When it came to deciding upon an architect, there was only one realistic choice.

Alexander Ross of Inverness was born in 1834, attended the Inverness Royal Academy and Bell's Institution. After a period as assistant he took over his deceased father's practice at the age of nineteen and from then on was to develop the church building side of his father's business.

With a succession of partners he was soon to gain a formidable reputation. Probably his greatest achievement was **St Andrews Cathedral, Inverness** (1866) but his numerous designs all over Scotland included mansions, police houses, banks, schools and churches of all denominations. His first solo achievement was **Geddes Mill** (1853) in Avoch designed when he was only nineteen. The **Mackenzie Foundation Episcopal School** in Avoch followed in 1864 and he was also responsible for its extension in 1890. In 1875 he built the **school and schoolhouse** in Courthill Road, Rosemarkie, and the following year redesigned **Rosemarkie Church and Manse**.

Ross's social connections were widened by his enlistment in the Volunteers at the Inverness Garrison Artillery of which he became colonel and still further by his entry into the ancient Masonic Lodge in Inverness known as 'Old Inverness Kilwinning St John's' which has been in existence since 1678 and probably earlier. He would most certainly have come to know Spence Ross who had also been a member.

He therefore was the natural choice for the new building that Spence Ross, his bishop and congregation envisaged at St Andrews. He presented his designs to the Managers.

They were not to be disappointed.

The Baptistry

There are no precise records of how and when the chancel were built but it must have been under discussion when in May 1904, Spence Ross informed the Managers that the Munros of Poyntzfield had asked permission to erect a Baptismal Font in memory of the late Captain and Mrs Munro and their son Frank who had been killed in the South African campaign. This was approved, Alexander Ross consulted and the Baptistry completed a year later.

Described as *an extraordinarily intimate space,* the style of the semi-octagonal Baptistry echoes that of the chancel as do the form of the windows. The theme of the central curvilinear rose window with its three worshipping angels reflects that of the central altar window. Here the Holy Spirit, symbolic of Baptism, is depicted as a Dove.

In the centre of the rose window, the tiny colourful inset inspired by the diocesan seal shows St Peter and St Boniface, to whom the neighbouring cathedral was dedicated. St Boniface, in this case, was the name given to (or taken by) the Celtic St Curadan, who built the first stone church (as opposed to wood) in the Roman tradition (as opposed to Celtic) in Rosemarkie and dedicated it to St Peter in 716 CE. (St Curadan in fact built four of these churches dedicated to St Peter. The other three are in the Aberdeen and Angus area) As this small inset is so unusual in style and content, some have wondered if it might be a relic of glass rescued from the ruined cathedral. A happy thought indeed. (See frontispiece).

The side windows depict the Baptism of Christ in the River Jordan and the Woman at the Well receiving the Water of Life. The beautiful stone tracery and the stained glass windows were gifted by Mrs H.H. Kennedy of Dunain Park, Inverness

The **Statue of the Virgin Mary and Child** was gifted in the early nineteen sixties by the widow of a Glasgow surgeon called Marshall in his memory. It was first placed at the chancel gates but caused such controversy among the congregation of the time that it was moved several times. It now stands, properly hallowed, in the Baptistry.

Although there is no mention of it in the records, the **porch** was probably added at about this time. The stained-glass window showing Queen Margaret of Scotland (1046-1093) in the act of feeding the poor was gifted by Spence Ross and his family. The symbolism perhaps represents all of humanity in need of the sustenance that only the Church sacraments can provide.

The Chancel

By 1906 the Managers were having cold feet over the erection of the Chancel. A new heating system was required and the insurance for the Church already risen to £1000 a year with a further £100 required for the Church Hall.

Although the church was now debt free, Spence Ross as treasurer reported that there were three sums of money belonging to the church which amounted to only £21 16/11d The estimate for the Chancel was £482. Mr Ross was consulted. Could he do it for less? He could not. Suddenly, or so it seems, the Managers changed their mind. It may have been the result of a spectacular Summer Bazaar or the fact that gifts had begun to pour in. In November 1906 the managers unanimously gave their permission to go ahead with the Chancel.

The plan included a three-sided apse with *sedilia,* (stone seating) and *piscina* (stone basin), south of the east-facing altar with an *aumbry* (tabernacle) and a recessed niche representing the Holy Sepulchre to the north. The latter is used today to house the Bishop's Chair. The *lympanum* of the recess bears a moulding of the diocesan seal of the Bishops of Ross, (St Peter and St Boniface/Curadan).

The woman at the well. One of the Baptistry windows

Among the many gifts, the carved oak Altar and Reredos with its representation of the last supper was presented by Mrs Travers of Bridge of Allan in memory of her brothers, Major-General Donald MacIntyre VC and General Ian MacIntyre one of whom lived next door north-west of the church at Mackenzie Lodge (burned down during the last war) and Meadowbank opposite the Church Hall. Both men had been active Managers of St Andrews and generous supporters of the improvements. A descendant still owns the little cottage in Academy Street which had once belonged to their coachman, George Scopes. He himself was a sidesman at St Andrews and, on one occasion, deputed to chase goats off the church green!

Windows

The beautiful rose window above the Altar was given by Miss Milne-Miller in memory of the late Surgeon-Major Milne-Miller of Kincurdie, Rosemarkie. It depicts Christ the King in glory surrounded by six angels. The two windows above the north end of the east-facing altar, gifted by the Mackenzies of Flowerburn, shows Faith and Hope together, and, in the other, Charity, as the most important of the three, leading a child. Above the south end of the altar the two windows gifted by Colonel Bruce Raikes Hall show Christ perhaps in the act of healing as he looks towards the Roman Centurion who is asking him to cure his servant, claiming that he was 'not worthy that Jesus should enter under his roof'. Christ is recognisable in stained glass by the scarlet robe of a martyr symbolising his suffering, and his halo which contains a cross. There are four types of halo. Medieval congregations could tell at a glance the importance of the figure by the colour of the robe and the content of the halo. Note the intertwined symbol of the Alpha and the Omega in the small light at the top of the rose window with the Lamb of God and the Burning Bush in the top lights above the side windows.

The **Nave Window** representing Christ the Good Shepherd and Christ the Light of the World in the two upper lights with St John and St Andrew below, was presented at a later date by the Haldane family who lived at St Katherines, Fortrose. Mrs Haldane, the widow of L S Haldane WS, was one of the two first woman members of the Vestry when in 1922 the Constitution was changed to include women and the Board of Management replaced by a Vestry.

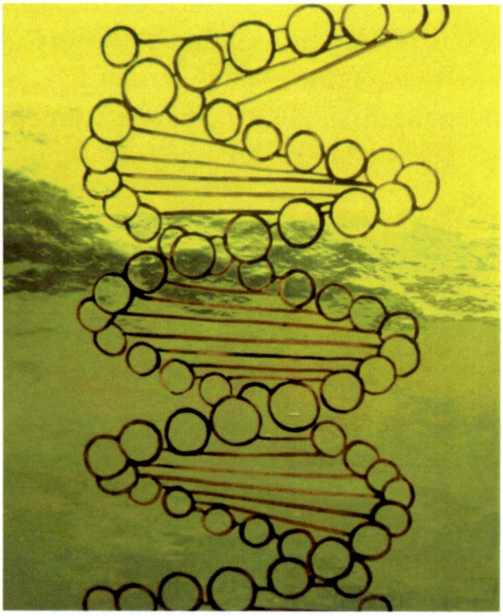

One of the more recent gifts is the image of the Double Helix as a symbol of life represented in the **Pulpit Window,** placed there in memory of Dr Grenville A. Robinson, a scientist and church office bearer who worked at the cutting edge of modern science.

The Stations of the Cross and Altar Crucifix

The fourteen small enamelled pictures that adorn the walls of the nave tell of Christ's final journey through the streets of Jerusalem, the *Via Dolorosa*, to Calvary, the scene of his Crucifixion. These were given by the Revd A.C. Buchanan, rector during the war years from 1939-1944. The Crucifix that hangs above the altar, attached to the top of the reredos was gifted by Miss Jean (Sine) Stuart of Angel Court on the same occasion.

The Pulpit and Lectern

The stone pulpit carved with its symbols of Christ as the Lamb of God and the entwined Greek letters, Alpha and Omega, symbolic of God as the first and last, was gifted by the family of the late A. G. Mackenzie, founder of the Mackenzie Foundation school in Avoch.

There have been several lecterns over the years from the brass eagle (long gone) which came from Colonel Stephen of Avoch House to the present one made by the wood-carver David Robinson and gifted as recently as 2013 by the family of Barbara Cameron, an office bearer and thirteen times a pilgrim to Santiago De Compostella.

Gifts

Other gifts poured in at the time and over the years too numerous to mention. They included vestments, one of which is believed to have belonged to the hymnist and theologian, John Mason Neale (1818-1866), a jewelled Altar Cross (now in St Johns Arpafeelie) and a set of silver Communion Vessels presented by James Douglas Fletcher of Rosehaugh. The oak altar rail and standards were gifted by St Johns Church, Forres. The Sanctuary Lamp and lamp for the porch (no electricity in the church till 1933) were presented by two locals, a Mrs Hodgson and a Mr Mackenzie. The brass alms dish still used was gifted by Mrs Neil Scobie of Hawkhill (better known to us today as Marine House, Rosemarkie). The colourful kneelers were designed and embroidered over a period of ten years from 1975, by members of the Work Party, a popular organisation for the women of the congregation started by Mrs Doris Dobson in the early fifties. A silver ciborium was presented by the Norwegian Brigade in 1944 as a token of gratitude for the use of the church during the war. More recent gifts include a Pulpit Bible, carpets, a banner of St Andrew, a garden seat and in 2016, altar linen and a wrought iron votive candle stand. In fact everything you see in St Andrews today was gifted, replaced or renewed with love and gratitude by friends and members of the congregation over the years.

The Consecration

On May 31 1909 at the AGM, Spence Ross informed his congregation that the Chancel, Baptistry and Porch were now completed and as the church was debt free it could therefore be consecrated. The ladies of the congregation under the convener-ship of Mrs Mackenzie of Flowerburn, Rosemarkie, were asked to arrange a luncheon for the Bishop, visiting clergy and guests .The service was duly held at 11 am on Wednesday August 25, 1909, and that date is remembered and celebrated every year.

Disaster

Few churches have escaped the sickly fingers of dry rot and St Andrews was not to be one of them. In 1911 the Managers entertained the idea of letting the Church Green to the Fortrose Tennis Club for £3 per annum in order to pay the Rose Street Iron Foundry for repairing the heating system (again!). The congregation voted against the Tennis Club and at the same time dry rot was discovered in the floor and in the wooden panelling around the walls of the nave and choir. Everything had to be taken out and burned. The cost of this and providing an entire new floor including spraying the walls with disinfectant came to over thirty pounds. Itwas decided not to replace the panelling. The old white-wash was removed and the walls pointed where necessary. They are precisely as you see them today. Over the years there have been other outbreaks of dry rot but never quite so disastrous as the first.

Pulpit Rail and Rood Screen

In 1912 it was noted by the Managers that Spence Ross, now seventy, had been with the congregation for over thirty years. To relieve him of some of his duties, a secretary and treasurer were appointed and for safety reasons it was decided that the pulpit stair needed a rail. Again Mrs Kennedy came to the rescue. Not only did she pay for the handsome brass rail but also provided new psalters and hymn books, a chancel screen and sanctuary carpet.

Organ Chamber and Vestry

Spence Ross had however not finished with his improvements but it was not until 1913 that the Managers could contemplate the addition of a vestry and organ chamber. The congregation was approached to hold another Grand Bazaar in what was then the Drill Hall in Fortrose (now St Peter and St Boniface Roman Catholic Church). The estimate came to £320, enough money was raised and building duly commenced. At the same time a church cleaner was engaged for five shillings a month and the ladies put in charge of the soft furnishings. This included new matting for the aisle while the old matting would have to do for the new vestry. Both were completed before the onset of war and a fence erected between Academy Street and the church green with a gate at the north-east corner (no doubt to keep out the goats!)

The Organ

The names of various organists are recorded over those early years including that of the second Mrs Spence Ross, and the borrowed 'American organ' which had served the congregation for many years was still in use. The new organ chamber, however, required a proper pipe organ. In 1915 Lady Gordon Cumming offered, for the price of its removal, the pipe organ in use in Altyre Chapel. After due inspection the organ was accepted with thanks, installed and insured for £359. The 'American organ' was gratefully returned to Rosehaugh House.

Although second-hand, the pipe organ survived until 2007 when congregational contributions hugely and generously supplemented by the late Patrick Zentler-Munro, a senior consultant at Raigmore Hospital and

Old Organ Pipes re-used in the new hybrid Organ

himself a talented organist. He enabled St Andrews to install a splendid new digitally-enhanced instrument which was consecrated by the Bishop on February 17, 2008.

This freed the old organ chamber which was furnished and put to use as a quiet room for robing, prayer and meditation groups. Though it is not mentioned in the minutes, the windows suggest that Spence Ross had perhaps intended it as a Lady Chapel similar to St Regulus in Cromarty.

The Great War

Both General Hunter-Blair and Admiral Lowry commanding the Northern District were in touch with Spence Ross regarding the black-out of the church. Blinds were briefly contemplated and dismissed. Instead it was decided to hold Evensong at 3 pm in the winter months.

The Rector Retires

In May 1917 at the AGM held in the Church Hall, Spence Ross, now a Canon of Inverness Cathedral, announced his decision to retire. He was 75 yeas old. He had not only been responsible for the extensive improvements of St Andrews but had also overseen the building of St Regulus in Cromarty. Mr John Mackenzie, the Rector's Warden and oldest member of the congregation recalled *Canon Ross's long connection with the Church, his arduous, zealous, and successful labours, his broadly-sympathetic visiting, the sums he raised for buildings such as the Church at Cromarty, the Church with its additions at Fortrose, the Church Hall at Fortrose etc. and he referred to the Canon's great energy and unfailing performance of duty through many years of difficulty which made possible a great extension of work at Cromarty and won the admiration and esteem not only of those to whom he had ministered but of many outside Church membership.*

Although officially retired, the Canon by no means relinquished his interest in St Andrews. He remained a vestry member and took all the services during the various *inter-regna* until his death in 1929. He was buried in the Fortrose cathedral just behind where the high altar had once stood and is remembered by a handsome stone plaque in St Andrews church which was erected by the local Masonic Lodge of which he had been a founder member.

On St Andrews centenary in 2009, his great grandson, Richard West, presented a silver salver to the church which had once belonged to his forebear. It is in use at every Eucharist.

The Rectory

After Spence Ross's retirement, the new rector, one of three Englishmen who had been interviewed for the post, the Revd John Anthony Lombe Atthill MA (Cantab) from Bedford, was unanimously chosen by the congregation and instituted in November 1918 at a stipend of £80 pa. Where, though, was he to live? The Spence Ross family still occupied the schoolhouse in Avoch. (The school was not to close until 1930, a year after Spence Ross's death.)

The Fletchers of Rosehaugh had offered the **Deanery** but it was already occupied by sitting tenants, (the unmarried daughters of the late explorer, Alexander Mackenzie of Canada). **Angel Court** in Rose Street was vacant so the congregation held a *Cafe Chantant* and Produce Sale in the Drill Hall to raise money for the rent. Angel Court then was sold and in 1923 the vestry purchased ***Bon Accord*** (now called Brae House).

Unfortunately half of *Bon Accord* was already occupied by a farmer, Tom Macdonald, who operated his dairy business from the door so it was not considered satisfactory. It was finally sold to the sitting tenant for £850 while the Vestry once again was in search of a permanent rectory

In 1931, Mrs Fletcher of Rosehaugh, now a widow, formally gifted the **Deanery,** tenant-free to the Bishop (not the Vestry). Although a beautiful old house it was in a bad state of repair and needed a new kitchen and bathroom wing. According to the Registers, it was to become from then on a constant source of anxiety and debt to the congregation.

By 1967 evidence of dry rot was found in the drawing-room and there was an infestation of woodworm. The cost of maintaining an old building and the discomfort of living in the unheated house prompted Bishop Macinnes (technically the owner) to insist that the reluctant Vestry arrange to sell the Deanery to someone who could afford the cost of repairs, heating and upkeep. A new custom-built rectory was planned for the foot of the garden. The trauma was great but the Vestry members efficient and supportive and the new house and garage finished by 1970. The **Deanery** was sold for £7500 and the new Rectory at 1 Deans Road with garage completed for £7814.

The Services

We tend to think as we grow older that everything in the past life of our church was different, certainly bigger and probably better! Comparisons are odious as we well know but sometimes it's interesting to look back and see how the services and attendances in those far off days compare with today.

Several facts stand out. For example **Evensong** was the best-attended service in the 'twenties and 'thirties. The numbers are surprising. Fortrose was a much smaller place in those days yet there were seldom less that 30 in the evening and during Father Magnus Laing's ministry (1926-30), seldom less than 50 and often as many as 80! The Fleet was anchored in the Cromarty Firth at that time and this may have accounted for the numbers but there is no mention of it in the Register.

The nationwide decline in numbers attending Evensong used to be associated with the BBC's showing of *The Forsyte Saga* on Sunday evening television in the late 'fifties but, looking at the Register, the decline started during the war. Perhaps this was partly due to the fact that the evening service times were continually changing to accommodate black-out conditions, and petrol was rationed.

Up until 1926, **Matins** was the main service on Sunday mornings with a shortened Holy Communion to follow on the second Sunday of the month. Thereafter **Sung Eucharist** became the main service on Sunday mornings at 11.30. This was the pattern until 1965. During the *inter-regnum* the congregation requested of Bishop Macinnes (who reluctantly agreed) that Matins be restored at 11.30 for three Sundays in the month with Holy Communion on the fourth. Whether it made any difference to the overall numbers attending is not known because during that period only communicant numbers were recorded. The alms-giving however increased considerably. Ten years later **Sung Eucharist** was restored and has remained the principal Sunday service. Numbers attending the main morning service when recorded fluctuated between 20 and 30 in the early 'twenties, 40 - 50 in the late twenties and thirties. 20-25 was the average during the war years rising to about 25-30 in the fifties though a good Sunday would see 40 and a poor winter Sunday as few as 12.

The time of the **early Communion** Sunday service fluctuated between 8, 8.30 and 9 but the numbers remained fairly consistent averaging 10 communicants. **Daily Mass** was held on five weekdays from 1930-1982 and there were few days when the rector was unable to celebrate due to no congregation.

Sunday School and **Bible Class** were only briefly and occasionally mentioned as resuming after school holidays but Father Laing was the first to start **Catechism** classes every Sunday at 3 pm. **Confirmations** were held usually but not always annually. The greatest number of candidates to be recorded was 19 in 1927. The fruits of that Confirmation were to have a lasting effect on St Andrews, the bedrock of congregations for decades to come.

Liturgy

Throughout the years since the Reformation the Scottish Episcopal Church has always had a Prayer Book. Gifts of Prayer Books, Bibles, Hymnals and pointed Psalm Books are recorded regularly in the Registers. 1929 was a milestone when the **Scottish Prayer Book** (the 'Red Book') was first compiled under the guidance of Bishop Maclean of Moray, Ross and Caithness. It was received with much joy and acclaim, described as *the pinnacle of achievement in the best of Anglican liturgical work.*

In 1966 and 1970 the first of the new Communion Liturgies appeared, to become known as the little 'Grey Book' (the printer had an excess of grey card!) Introduced slowly for congregations hate change, St Andrews had just become accustomed to it when in 1977 the 'Orange Book' appeared. This was the first of the modern language liturgies and was followed in 1982 by the 'Blue Book'. These changes to time-honoured language caused great angst in congregations all over Scotland, and St Andrews was no different. Passions were roused on both sides. A compromise was reached. In St Andrews the 'Grey Book' is still used at the 8 am Communion and midweek, a modern language version at 11 30 and the 1929 Scottish Prayer Book at Evensong.

Some of the Kneelers made by members of the congregation.

The reredos depicting the last supper

Previous Rectors

After Canon Spence Ross announced his retirement in 1918 there were between forty and fifty applicants for the charge. A small committee consisting of Mr Fletcher, Colonel Macdonald Smith and Mr Brayshaw, schoolmaster and lay reader, reduced the numbers to three who were invited to Rosehaugh to be interviewed.

John Anthony Lombe Athill 1918-1920

He had already been assisting Spence Ross in his last year before his appointment to the charge. A very young man, he had graduated from Selwyn College, Cambridge in 1912, attended the Edinburgh Theological College for a year and served two curacies in Ireland and in Herts before coming to the Black Isle. He seems to have had a restless nature for after two years he left Fortrose to spend a year in Dufftown followed by a year in Panama. In 1923 he was Diocesan Supernumerary in Aberdeen for three years followed by two years as rector of Fochabers. He then spent short periods in Natal, Brechin and Aberdeen before a call to Peebles in 1934 where he stayed until he retired in 1938.

Frederick Carlisle-Burton FRGS 1920-1925

A student of Chichester Theological College and a Fellow of the Royal Geographical Society, Father Carlisle-Burton was priested in 1889 in Grahamestone, S Africa. He served two curacies in Cape Colony and Port Elizabeth before becoming vicar of Adelaide in Cape Colony from 1891-1899. He then came to Scotland and after a short period in St Marks, Glasgow, was appointed rector of Girvan from 1904-1920. He and his Glasgow-born wife and eighteen year old son, Bede, then moved to Fortrose where they stayed in the *Bon Accord* rectory. A popular genial man he would no doubt have remained longer but was tragically knocked off his motor bike in Fortrose and killed in 1925. He is remembered by a plaque on the north nave wall of St Andrews. Both Father Athill and Father Carlyle-Burton were, like Canon Spence Ross, members of the local Masonic Lodge.

John Magnus Laing 1926-1930

A graduate of St John's Oxford and Ely Theological College, Father Laing served his curacy at St Saviours, Hoxton, from 1909-1920. After a year in the Bahamas he returned to St Mary's, Westminster, where he remained until he came to the Black Isle. Although he stayed for only four years, Father Laing's ministry was to have a profound and lasting effect on the congregation. A high Anglo-Catholic, he introduced more ritual to the services, and is remembered for having the largest Confirmation class ever recorded at St Andrews. Under his guidance, his Sunday School children saved their collection pennies and he sent their local young student teacher, Jean Hay, (later to become headmistress of Charles Edward Brooke's Church of England Girls School in Camberwell) all the way to London to choose and acquire the Crib figures still in use. For decades thereafter the

Church relied on the legacy of worship and loyalty that he inspired. He suffered from serious eye problems which required an operation and complete rest. He left Fortrose in 1930 to become vicar of Arlington in Sussex and died in 1949.

Archibald Kenneth Campbell 1930-1937

He attended St Chad's Durham. From 1922 he was a curate in London and in 1926 briefly converted to Roman Catholicism. Two years later he was received back into the Anglican Communion and until his appointment to Fortrose served as a curate in London. 'Archie' as he liked to be called by all had nine boy servers, was deeply involved in the Scout Movement particularly the first Chanonry Sea-Scouts and he also looked after the Cubs. He married Jean Douglass, granddaughter of Mrs Haldane of St Katherines and they were the first clergy family to live in the Deanery. Archie left Fortrose in 1937 to become Rector of Dunoon, He was made a Canon of Oban Cathedral in 1953 and retired in 1959. An enthusiast, he travelled round the seaside parishes to research and then publicise his book on sailing which was the love of his life.

John Baynham Windsor-Garnett 1937-1939

He attended Lichfield Theological College and served curacies in Staffordshire and Yorkshire and parishes in Dorset and Devon from 1922 until 1930 when he was appointed to Talham Fells in Lancashire where he remained until coming to Fortrose in 1937.

One of his servers, the late James Lumsden, remembered him *as a bachelor living with his mother in the Deanery, who did not involve himself in the community . Of a mild and retiring personality he seemed content to involve himself solely in the affairs of the church.*

Two anecdotes from his time have survived. Major Stuart who had bought Angel Court complained one morning that he was late for the early service. 'Only five minutes,' Father Windsor-Garnett excused himself. 'Five minutes at breakfast is half an hour by lunch time,' replied the Major sternly.

The other story is recorded from Avoch. The taxi driver who drove him to Cromarty every Sunday to take the weekly service at St Regulus remembered him as courteous and friendly. His family still possess the beautiful Bible given to them by him in gratitude when he left.

Alexander Cockburn Buchanan 1939-1944

Father Buchanan as he liked to be called served Fortrose and Cromarty during the war years He was remembered by James Lumsden as *a tall majestic person who loved walking and gave the impression of being a keep-fit enthusiast.* The Black Isle was a hive of activity during the war years, a restricted area full of soldiers, sailors and airmen billeted in the area and Father Buchanan a devoted pastor.

Lewis W.R.Hollowood 1944-1946

Father Hollowood, born in 1917, was only 27 when he came to Fortrose with his young wife having attended Edinburgh Theological College and two curacies served in Dundee and Chester. Full of enthusiasm, good with young people, he was unhappily plagued by ill-health and resigned after barely two years in the parish to become a Chaplain at Kings College Hospital in London.

Edgar J.P. Dobson 1946-1965

Canon Dobson was born in Greenock in 1898 and attended the Edinburgh Theological College in 1936 after nearly twenty years in the business world. He was a curate at St Margarets, Newlands, in Glasgow, then rector of Callander followed by Kirkcaldy before coming to Fortrose with his wife Doris and young family in 1946.

Small, latterly bearded, bent with arthritis, Canon Dobson soon became a recognisable figure as he sped around the Black Isle at an alarming speed in his soft-topped Morris 8. A dedicated and devoted priest, he was not above haranguing the faithful few from the pulpit for the absence of the rest and his Vestry for any perceived slackness. His skills lay in organisation and he was soon appointed Synod Clerk of the diocese, a Canon of Inverness Cathedral and a member of the Fortrose Town Council where he served as convener on several committees. His relaxation was bowling and he is remembered as a charming, delightful and enthusiastic person on the Green, eventually becoming club president.

Like Spence Ross, his talents were many. Witty, with great powers of mimicry and a born raconteur, Canon Dobson could also be formidable. His wife, Doris, on the other hand, though equally capable and hard-working, hid her many talents under a gentle and always kind exterior. Among her many activities she started, hosted and organised the St Andrews Work Party, played the organ and was a founder member of the Fortrose Branch of the SWRI.

One of Canon Dobson's first duties was to help officiate at the wedding of his self- chosen successor, John Marshall.

John Dixon Marshall 1965-1974

Born in 1917, John Marshall was also the product of the Edinburgh Theological College having received his vocation as a chorister in Shanghai Cathedral before the war. After four yeas as a curate at Old St Pauls, Edinburgh he then became an Army Chaplain serving in Kenya, Mogadishu and the RAMC depot near Aldershot. In 1953 he was appointed a minor canon and a year later precentor at Ripon Cathedral Anxious to return to the Scottish Episcopal Church he accepted an invitation to become rector of St Olafs in Kirkwall, followed by six years at St Peters, Galashiels, before his appointment to Fortrose in 1965.

Father John's greatest talent lay in music. He was an accomplished organist and pianist. Being a people person he was elected, like Canon Dobson, a member of the Town Council. He started summer services at St Johns, Arpafeelie, which had been unused for many years and he encouraged ecumenism locally by sharing the pulpit (literally!) on many occasions with his Church of Scotland brethren in Fortrose and Cromarty. During his incumbency the Vestry was advised by Bishop Macinnes to sell the Deanery. His was the first family to occupy the new custom-built rectory at the foot of the old garden.

After nearly ten years in Fortrose, Father John was appointed rector of St John the Evangelist, Baillieston, and St Serfs, Shettleston, in the east end of Glasgow where he remained for a further nine years until his retirement in 1982 when he and his wife returned to live in Rosemarkie.

Iain William Thomas Duff McHardy 1974-1980

Canon McHardy attended St Andrews University followed by Ely Theological College and served curacies in South Kirby and Cantley before his appointment to St Ninians, Invergordon, where he remained for twenty-two years. Much interested in local politics he also served as Provost of Invergordon Town Council and became Synod Clerk to the Diocese. Multi-talented, gentle and wise, with a great love for children, he started the Adventurers, a popular Christian organisation for all interested Fortrose children. He also re-designed and improved the delapidating Church Hall. Father Iain came to St Andrews as a Canon then in 1977 was appointed Dean of the Diocese. He too retired to the Black Isle where he was able to expand his interest in amateur radio.

John Alexander Howard 1981-1994

John Howard attended the College of the Resurrection, Mirfield, served his curacy in Almondbury and was Vicar of Skelmanthorpe before his appointment to St Andrews where he remained until his retirement. One of his finest achievements was to restore St Johns, Arpafeelie, into the flourishing congregation it is today, making it once more viable for worship with heating and lighting and regular services. He was also responsible for the formation of the 1st Fortrose Boys Brigade Company which was attached to St Andrews. A deeply caring man, he was a tireless evangelist and ecumenist. During his ministry two men were inspired to join the priesthood and his eldest son followed him into the ministry. He and his wife Marjorie retired to Oxfordshire in 1994.

Richard Francis Burkitt 1995-2008

Richard attended Leeds University, and worked as a teacher and an inner city youth worker in Leeds for ten years before attending Salisbury and Wells Theological College. Priested in 1990, he was curate at Cavendish, then rector of Fraserburgh and New Pitsligo before his appointment to the Black Isle. Like Spence Ross, Richard is an enthusiast especially supportive of the disadvantaged, the depressed and the needy. A tireless worker among the young of Fortrose, his youth club and drama group and monthly Family Services on Sunday mornings were a source of inspiration to many. His love for cricket involved him in getting to know several young heroin addicts in Inverness. After thirteen years he left Fortrose to start his own charity in Inverness to support those recovering from addiction not only to drugs but also alcohol and prescription pills. Today **For The Right Reasons** runs a charity shop and a flourishing print and publishing business in the Merkinch district of Inverness.

St Andrews Today

In 2009, the anniversary year of its consecration, St Andrews together with the congregations of St Regulus, Cromarty, and St John the Evangelist, Arpafeelie, became legally under Constitution the joint **Black Isle Charge**. The first meeting of the joint Vestry together with their rector, Canon Mel Langille, took place on the 31 March under the chairmanship of the Bishop of the Diocese of Moray, Ross and Caithness. The three congregations join each other in turn for worship on the fifth Sunday in the month and the rector divides his time between the three churches and their members. The three buildings are always open and visitors made very welcome.

The **Church Hall** now houses a remarkably popular Charity Shop open on Wednesday and Saturday mornings and run by members of the three congregations. This and other fund-raising events held over the years have enabled the Black Isle Parish to support a priest and help pay for the upkeep of five buildings.

The secular history of St Andrews as described in the old Registers is like that of most other churches, a leaking roof, wet rot in the porch, perishing window lead, mice at the candles, fire in the vestry, dangerous finials, little and not such little disasters that afflict all buildings from time to time over the years.

Today St Andrews is a living and inclusive Church tended by faithful hands, beautified by generous hearts and led by devoted shepherds. Built, metaphorically speaking, brick by brick on the prayers of its members, past and present, it aims to be part of a vital and ongoing ministry. St Andrews is also a place of communication with one all-important story to tell - the good news of the Gospel of Christ. Here you will find in this little welcoming world, a small oasis of refreshment and peace.

First and foremost, however, St Andrews is a place of worship hallowed by the ever-present Sacrament and daily prayer, yours included, where the barriers of busy-ness, stress and sadness no longer loom so large. Heaven seems just that bit closer.

Failte gu. You are very welcome.

Deo gratias.

In the 1920's, as a young girl, Jean Hay, (later to become headmistress of Charles Edward Brooke's Church of England Girls School in Camberwell) went all the way to London to choose and acquire the Crib figures still in use. See page 19.

EVERYTHING YOU NEED TO KNOW ABOUT

TAYLOR SWIFT

WELCOME

Taylor Swift signed her first record deal when she was just 14. Since then she has revolutionised the music industry, sold millions of albums worldwide breaking multiple records and amassed an army of fans. If you're a Swiftie, this is the perfect book for you. Inside you'll find everything you need to know about the superstar from where her journey started to her meteoric rise to fame, her life and relationships, challenges and triumphs. Discover what makes her a fashion guru, inspiration and icon whose name will go down in history.

FUTURE

EVERYTHING YOU NEED TO KNOW ABOUT

TAYLOR SWIFT

Future PLC Quay House, The Ambury, Bath, BA1 1UA

Editorial
Editor **Zara Gaspar**
Designer **Perry Wardell-Wicks**
Senior Art Editor **Andy Downes**
Head of Art & Design **Greg Whitaker**
Editorial Director **Jon White**

Contributors
Rebecca Bradbury; Jo Cole

Cover images
Getty images

Photography
All copyrights and trademarks are recognised and respected

Advertising
Media packs are available on request
Commercial Director **Clare Dove**

International
Head of Print Licensing **Rachel Shaw**
licensing@futurenet.com
www.futurecontenthub.com

Circulation
Head of Newstrade **Tim Mathers**

Production
Head of Production **Mark Constance**
Production Project Manager **Matthew Eglinton**
Advertising Production Manager **Joanne Crosby**
Digital Editions Controller **Jason Hudson**
Production Managers **Keely Miller, Nola Cokely, Vivienne Calvert, Fran Twentyman**

Printed in the UK

Distributed by Marketforce, 5 Churchill Place, Canary Wharf, London, E14 5HU
www.marketforce.co.uk – For enquiries, please email:
mfcommunications@futurenet.com

EYNTKA Taylor Swift First Edition (MUB5310)

FUTURE

Connectors.
Creators.
Experience
Makers.

Future plc is a public company quoted on the London Stock Exchange (symbol: FUTR)
www.futureplc.com

Chief Executive Officer **Jon Steinberg**
Non-Executive Chairman **Richard Huntingford**
Chief Financial and Strategy Officer **Penny Ladkin-Brand**

Tel +44 (0)1225 442 244

Widely Recycled

ipso. For press freedom with responsibility

CONTENTS

Gibson

TAYLOR SWIFT

FROM A CHRISTMAS TREE FARM TO THE GLOBAL STAGE, DISCOVER HOW IT ALL STARTED

MGM

Taylor Alison Swift was born on 13 December 1989 in West Reading, Pennsylvania. Some may say that Taylor's parents manifested their daughter's career path by naming her after the legendary singer-songwriter James Taylor, but music was already in her blood. Taylor was inspired to sing by her maternal grandmother, who was a professional opera singer. Recognise the name Marjorie from Taylor's *evermore* album? This track is Taylor's tribute to her late grandma.

Image: Michael Buckner / Getty images

SOME MAY SAY THAT TAYLOR'S PARENTS MANIFESTED THEIR DAUGHTER'S CAREER PATH BY NAMING HER AFTER JAMES TAYLOR, BUT MUSIC WAS ALREADY IN THE BLOOD

After spending her early childhood on an 11-acre farm in Reading, Pennsylvania, Taylor moved with her mum, dad and brother to Wyomissing, where they rented this five-bedroom property on Grandview Boulevard. At 11 years old, Taylor joined the local junior high, but has since spoken about how hard she found it to fit in at school during this period of her life.

Image: MediaNews Group / Getty images

ONE OF THE MOST BEAUTIFUL THEMES TAYLOR EXPLORES IN HER SONGWRITING IS HER RELATIONSHIP WITH HER MUM

One of the most beautiful themes Taylor explores in her songwriting is the relationship she shares with her mum, Andrea Swift. A former marketing manager, Andrea has always stood by her daughter and remains part of her close team. In *Miss Americana*, Taylor's 2020 Netflix documentary, the singer describes Andrea as her 'favourite person in the world'.

Image: Denise Truscello / Getty images

In 2015, Andrea was sadly diagnosed with breast cancer. Taylor revealed the disease had returned in an essay she wrote for *Elle* magazine in 2019. During Andrea's treatment, a brain tumour was also discovered. Reflecting on these experiences, Taylor penned a song about her mum's cancer battle called 'Soon You'll Get Better', which featured on her 2019 album, *Lover*.

Image: Rick Kern / Getty images

Did you know?

THE FIRST SONG TAYLOR LEARNT TO PLAY ON THE GUITAR WAS 'KISS ME' BY SIXPENCE NONE THE RICHER. BETTER KNOWN FOR THEIR ALTERNATIVE ROCK SOUND, THE BAND PROVIDED A SLIGHTLY DIFFERENT SORT OF INSPIRATION FOR TAYLOR, WHO CITES HER ROLE MODELS AS THE COUNTRY MUSIC ARTISTS LEANN RHIMES, SHANIA TWAIN AND THE DIXIE CHICKS. IT WAS AFTER WATCHING A DOCUMENTARY ABOUT FAITH HILL THAT TAYLOR BECAME SURE SHE NEEDED TO MOVE TO NASHVILLE TO PURSUE HER DREAMS. SHE ALSO HAD THE FORESIGHT FROM A VERY YOUNG AGE TO KNOW SHE NEEDED TO OFFER THE INDUSTRY SOMETHING DIFFERENT, WHICH IS WHY SHE PICKED UP THE GUITAR AND STARTED WRITING HER OWN MUSIC.

INSTEAD OF GIVING AN INTERVIEW SHE CONTRIBUTED A POEM

Taylor is also close to her dad, Scott Kingsley Swift, a former stockbroker who the singer describes as 'a big teddy bear who tells me everything I do is perfect'. In 2004, when Taylor was just 14 years old, he transferred to his firm's Nashville office and relocated to the city with his family so Taylor could be closer to the song-writing opportunities the Tennessee capital offered.

Image: Charley Gallay / Stringer / Getty images

But Taylor began dedicating songs to her family far earlier than this. Back in 2008, the singer included the song 'The Best Day' on her second album, *Fearless*. The lyrics pay tribute to her mum, dad and brother (picture above), and recall childhood memories of pumpkin patches and tractor rides.

Image: Gardiner Anderson/Bauer-Griffin / Getty images

Fun Fact

TAYLOR DOESN'T SOLELY USE HER UNRIVALLED WRITING SKILLS FOR CRAFTING LYRICS AND SIGNING AUTOGRAPHS. WHEN THE STAR WAS IN 4TH GRADE, SHE WON A NATIONAL POETRY CONTEST WITH A POEM CALLED 'MONSTER IN MY CLOSET'. WE CAN ONLY ASSUME THE STAR HAS CONTINUED TO PEN POETRY ALONGSIDE WRITING SONGS, AS IN 2017 SHE APPEARED ON THE COVER OF BRITISH *VOGUE*, BUT INSTEAD OF GIVING AN INTERVIEW SHE CONTRIBUTED HER OWN POEM CALLED 'THE TRICK TO HOLDING ON'. SHE'S ALSO OPENED UP ABOUT WRITING AN UNPUBLISHED NOVEL WHEN SHE WAS JUST 14 YEARS OLD CALLED *A GIRL CALLED GIRL*.

Image: Kevin Mazur / Getty Images

TAYLOR SWIFT

When Taylor first arrived on the music scene she was rarely seen without a pair of cowboy boots. The footwear of choice for many country stars, they signify the singer's musical roots. Not only did she grow up listening to the genre, but she also began crafting her own country songs as a young teen. For two hours after school every Tuesday she would have writing sessions with the lyricist Liz Rose, who would become one of Taylor's long-term writing partners.

Image: Rusty Russell / Getty images

Taylor's headshot now adorns a wall inside the iconic Bluebird Cafe alongside signed photographs of other country songwriters who have also performed at the in-the-round venue. The success of her first few albums catapulted country into mainstream and introduced a new audience of younger fans to the genre.

Image: Robert Alexander / Getty images

Austin Kingsley Swift is Taylor's only sibling. Three years younger than his sister, he reportedly has fond memories of childhood holidays spent in their parent's Jersey beach house together. After a stint of studying photography in college, he switched to acting and graduated from the University of Notre Dame in Indiana in 2015. Since then he's had roles in sitcoms and films, including *Braking for Whales* and *We Summon the Darkness*.

Image: Rick Diamond / Getty images

It was an industry showcase at the Bluebird Cafe, a local Austin music venue, that led to Taylor getting signed by Big Machine Records. It was 2005 – a year after Taylor turned down a development deal with Sony/ATV as she felt the firm didn't value her song-writing abilities. Big Machine Records, on the other hand, was a new, independent record label set up by Scott Borchetta, which would offer Taylor more control over her musical direction.

Image: Robert Alexander / Getty images

Did you know?

IF TAYLOR LIKES ANYTHING MORE THAN MAKING MUSIC, IT'S HER THREE GORGEOUS PEDIGREE CATS. THE ELDEST IS A TABBY SCOTTISH FOLD CALLED MEREDITH GREY, NAMED AFTER THE PROTAGONIST IN TV SHOW *GREY'S ANATOMY*. NEXT UP IS ANOTHER SCOTTISH FOLD CALLED OLIVA BENSON, NAMED AFTER THE LEAD CHARACTER IN *LAW AND ORDER: SVU*. OLIVIA HAS EVEN FEATURED IN ONE OF TAYLOR'S DIET COKE COMMERCIALS, AS WELL AS HER VIDEO FOR 'BLANK SPACE'. THE YOUNGEST CAT IS A BLUE-EYED RAGDOLL NAMED BENJAMIN BUTTON, WHICH TAYLOR ADOPTED AFTER HE FEATURED IN HER MUSIC VIDEO FOR 2019'S 'ME!' WITH PANIC! AT THE DISCO'S BRENDON URIE.

Image: Kevin Mazur / Getty Images

Taylor began taking guitar lessons with local computer repairman and part-time musician Ronnie Cremer when she was around 12 years old. He would come to Taylor's house twice a week to teach her chords and help her write songs. The singer is now also a master of the banjo, ukulele and piano, as seen in many of her live performances.

Image: Mark Humphrey / Getty images

The first single Taylor released was 'Tim McGraw', a song about a summer romance coming to an end, which references the country artist in the chorus. The idea came to Taylor while in maths class and she finessed the song after school with Liz Rose. Taylor has since performed with Tim and opened for him in 2007, as part of his world tour with his wife, Faith Hill.

Image: Frederick Breedon IV / Getty images

Taylor is seen here with her brother attending an American football game in 2010, a decade or so after making some of her first performances at sports events. Her first major gig was at just 11 years old, when she sang the US national anthem at a Philadelphia 76ers basketball game. And when it comes to NFL, Taylor's a big Philadelphia Eagles fan.

Image: Sipa US / Alamy Stock Photo

Swifties will no doubt know that Taylor spent her early childhood growing up on a Christmas tree farm, with her love of the festive season reflected in her music. Here is Taylor in 2007, when she performed at the Rockefeller Tree Lighting Ceremony in New York City. She has also penned original Christmas songs, added holiday-inspired lyrics to songs such as 'Lover' and is even said to incorporate festive decorations into her birthday celebrations on 13th December every year.

Image: Kevin Mazur / Getty images

FEARLESS

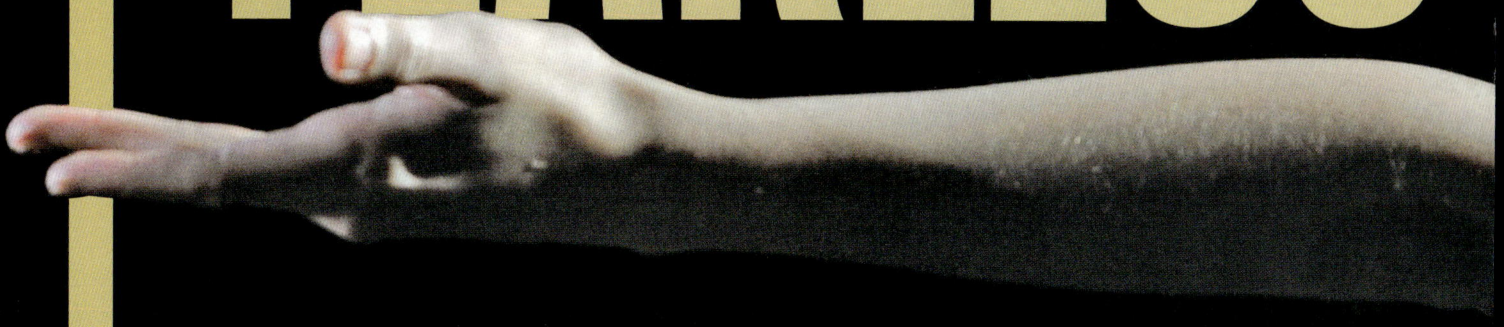

WHETHER IT'S SPEAKING HER TRUTH IN SONG LYRICS OR STANDING UP TO INDUSTRY POWERHOUSES, THERE IS NO SUPERSTAR AS COURAGEOUS AS TAYLOR SWIFT

Taylor knew she had to stand out amid the Nashville music scene in order to get a record deal, so she learnt to play the guitar and started writing her own songs. Her daring paid off, as she harnessed her natural song-writing abilities and discovered a way to express her thoughts and emotions. Here she is performing with her personalised guitar on her first tour in 2007.

Image: Jason Moore / Alamy images

Even as a teenager, Taylor proved she was fearless. At 13 years old, she had the courage to pitch herself to record labels. Pictured here in 2006, the year her debut album was released, she has since explained the source of her bravery: "It's because I could never feel the kind of rejection that I felt in middle school. Because in the music industry, if they're gonna say no to you, at least they're gonna be polite about it."

Image: John Shearer / WireImage

Taylor opened her Fearless Tour dressed in this now-iconic marching band ensemble. Explaining the name choice for her second album, she said: "Fearless is getting back up and fighting for what you want over and over again... It's fearless to have faith that someday things will change." Such determination encapsulates her approach to both her career and life in general.

Image: Jason Kempin / Getty images

TAYLOR KNEW SHE HAD TO STAND OUT, SO SHE LEARNT TO PLAY THE GUITAR AND STARTED WRITING HER OWN SONGS. HER DARING PAID OFF

Performing her single 'Should Have Said No' at the Academy of Country Music Awards in 2008, Taylor began wearing a hoodie and jeans before changing on stage into this little black dress. The lyrics are based on a conversation she had when confronting her cheating ex-boyfriend. Taylor makes it clear she'll never get back with him, providing an empowering message for listeners to have the confidence to know their self-worth – a message she continues to push to this day.

Image: Ethan Miller / Alamy images

This was the moment Taylor's high-profile feud with rapper Kanye West began. It was the 2009 MTV VMAs and Taylor was up on stage collecting the Best Female Video Award for 'You Belong With Me'. But mid-speech, Kanye stormed the stage, grabbed the mic and declared Beyonce should have won. What followed was a masterclass from Taylor on how to graciously forgive, stand up to bullies and have the fortitude to prove naysayers wrong.

Image: Kevin Mazur / WireImage / Getty images

WHAT FOLLOWED WAS A MASTERCLASS FROM TAYLOR ON HOW TO GRACIOUSLY FORGIVE AND STAND UP TO BULLIES

Did you know?

TAYLOR HAS PROVEN HER STRENGTH WHEN STANDING UP TO INDUSTRY BIG WIGS, AND WHEN IT COMES TO BEING WRONGED BY HER BEST MATES, SHE WILL SIMILARLY DEFEND HERSELF. CASE IN POINT IS THE 2014 TRACK 'BAD BLOOD', A SONG ABOUT BEING BETRAYED BY A CLOSE FRIEND. MANY BELIEVE THE SONG'S SUBJECT IS KATY PERRY AFTER THE PAIR ALLEGEDLY FELL OUT OVER SOME BACKING DANCERS. ALTHOUGH TAYLOR HAS DENIED THIS, THE WELL-KNOWN FEUD CAME TO AN END IN MAY 2018 WHEN KATY SENT TAYLOR A LITERAL OLIVE BRANCH AHEAD OF THE OPENING NIGHT OF HER REPUTATION TOUR. IN RETURN, TAYLOR SENT KATY SOME COOKIES ADORNED WITH FROSTING THAT SPELT 'PEACE AT LAST'.

Image: Clive Davis / Getty Images

Apologies can be a true sign of courage, which is something Taylor showcased in her track 'Back to December' from the album *Speak Now*. Performing the song here at the CMA Awards in 2010, the singer wrote the song as a remorseful plea to an ex-boyfriend. The entire album is about "figuring out how you feel and saying something about it".

Image: Rick Diamond / Getty images

IN RESPONSE TO KANYE'S RUDE INTERRUPTION, TAYLOR PENNED A SONG CALLED 'INNOCENT' FOR HER THIRD ALBUM

As this hug testifies, Taylor and Kanye had made peace by 2015. But it did not last long. He released a track the next year called 'Famous', which includes the lyrics: "I feel like me and Taylor might still have sex. Why? I made that b**** famous." The rapper then claimed Taylor gave the line her blessing – something the country star denied in a statement where she also called out his misogynistic language.

Image: Kevin Mazur / Getty images

Taylor poses here in 2012 with singer Rita Ora and reality TV star Kim Kardashian – Kanye West's ex-wife who also had a role to play in the public fallout. After the release of 'Famous' in 2016, Kim published footage appearing to show Taylor giving her approval of the lyrics. Four years later, the clip was proven to be edited, but at the time Taylor received a barrage of online hate, which contributed to her taking a prolonged break from the public eye.

Image: Dave Hogan / MTV / Getty images

In response to Kanye's rude interruption, Taylor penned a song called 'Innocent' for her third album, Speak Now. The lyrics of the gentle pop ballad sympathise with a man who has committed wrongdoings, demonstrating Taylor's boldness to forgive. She debuted the track at the 2010 MTV Video Music Awards, as pictured here.

Image: Kevin Mazur / Getty images

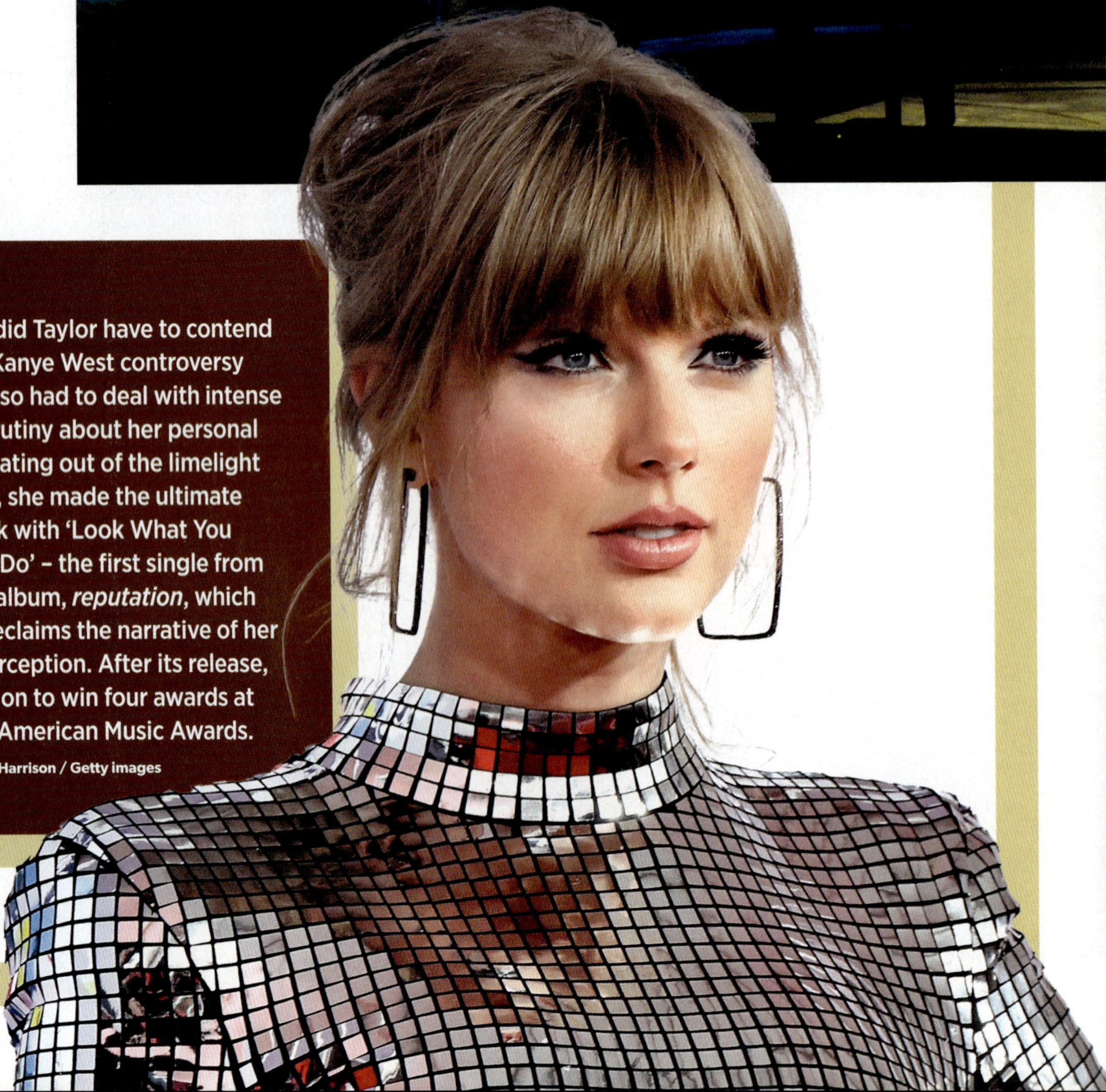

Not only did Taylor have to contend with the Kanye West controversy but she also had to deal with intense media scrutiny about her personal life. Retreating out of the limelight for a year, she made the ultimate comeback with 'Look What You Made Me Do' – the first single from her 2017 album, *reputation*, which bravely reclaims the narrative of her public perception. After its release, she went on to win four awards at the 2018 American Music Awards.

Image: Frazer Harrison / Getty images

Clad in a red sequined ringmaster costume, Taylor performs 'We Are Never Ever Getting Back Together' as part of her Red Tour. On the album *RED*, Taylor is unafraid to showcase all the messy emotions she's experienced in her love life, while the song '22' is Taylor flaunting her youth in the face of critics who previously dismissed her song-writing prowess because of her young age.

Image: Scott Barbour / TAS / Getty images

Performing the single 'Blank Space' with a golf club in hand was one of the most memorable images from Taylor's 1989 World Tour. The track is another tongue-in-cheek, self-referential response to the media's obsession with her love life and its portrayal of her, in her own words, as "a girl who's crazy but seductive but glamorous but nuts but manipulative".

Image: Steve Granitz / WireImage / Getty images

Taylor racked up many awards for her 2014 single 'Shake It Off', taken from her fifth studio album, *1989*. Inspired by her detractors, especially the tabloids, the song is Taylor's proactive, satirical stance to take back control of her public image. The lines "I go on too many dates / But I can't make 'em stay / At least that's what people say" is a takedown of the news outlets that portrayed her as a serial dater.

Image: Kevin Winter / Getty images

INSPIRED BY HER DETRACTORS, ESPECIALLY THE TABLOIDS, THE SONG IS TAYLOR'S PROACTIVE, SATIRICAL STANCE

While releasing multiple award-winning albums, Taylor was having to contend with a court case – which led to an office block opposite the courthouse in Denver making signs in support of the singer. It began in June 2013 when DJ David Mueller groped the singer while they were posing for a photo. After Taylor's team reported the incident to his employers, he was sacked from his job at KYGO radio station – a dismissal that caused him to file a lawsuit against Taylor for defamation.

Image: Joe Mahoney / Getty images

The handmade signs appeared when Taylor's counterclaim against Mueller went to court. The jury eventually ruled the DJ as guilty and Taylor was awarded a requested sum of $1. She also pledged to donate 'an unspecified amount' to organisations aimed at helping sexual assault victims. Going through such an ordeal under the public gaze is another sign of Taylor's fearlessness and strength, helping women find the courage to speak up against sexual harassment.

Image: Theo Stroomer / Getty images

Fun Fact

AFTER TAYLOR'S CIVIL CASE AGAINST MUELLER, SHE WAS NAMED ONE OF 'THE SILENCE BREAKERS' IN *TIME* MAGAZINE'S ANNUAL PERSON OF THE YEAR EDITION IN 2017. SHE SHARED THE FRONT COVER WITH FOUR OTHER WOMEN WHO WERE APPLAUDED FOR TELLING THEIR STORIES ABOUT SEXUAL ASSAULT AND HARASSMENT. THEY INCLUDE FORMER UBER EMPLOYEE SUSAN FOWLER WHO CALLED OUT SILICON VALLEY'S FRAT CULTURE AND ASHLEY JUDD, ONE OF THE FIRST WOMEN TO ACCUSE HARVEY WEINSTEIN OF SEXUAL HARASSMENT. YOU CAN ALSO SPOT A MYSTERY ARM IN THE BOTTOM RIGHT-HAND CORNER. THIS REPRESENTS THOSE WOMEN WHO ARE UNABLE TO SPEAK OUT DUE TO THE POTENTIALLY DIRE REPERCUSSIONS.

Image: Richard Levine / Alamy Images

Taylor is snapped here at an awards ceremony in 2015 with Scott Borchetta, the founder of Big Machine Records – the label the singer signed a 13-year deal with in 2006. On the surface all was well, but friction developed in 2018 when Taylor's contract ended and she switched to Universal's Republic Records, spurring a high-profile dispute about music ownership and artists' rights.

Image: Kevin Mazur / WireImage/ Getty images

Taylor high-fives her fans during the Tampa show of her Reputation Stadium Tour on 11 May 2018. The date marked the one-year anniversary of winning her civil case against Mueller, and she gave concert-goers an emotional speech reflecting on the trial and thanking her fans for their support throughout the ordeal. She also stressed the need for better justice for sexual assault victims.

Image: Kevin Mazur / Getty images

In an explosive Tumbler post, Taylor described Braun's buyout as her "worst case scenario", accusing him of "incessant, manipulative bullying" – after all, he had been working with Kanye West when the rapper slated her in his track 'Famous'. But Haim (pictured), Halsey and Iggy Azalea were among the musicians to publicly support Taylor over the controversy, applauding her willingness to speak out against industry figures as powerful as Braun in an effort to protect her work and artistry.

Image: Matt Winkelmeyer / VF23 / Getty images

◀ Months after Taylor's contract with Big Machine Records ended, the record label announced it had been acquired by music mega-manager Scooter Braun. Taylor had been trying to acquire her master recordings – the original recorded versions of her tracks – from Borchetta for years. But after refusing to budge, he had passed the ownership rights over to Braun, who would now profit every time a fan streamed or downloaded a Taylor Swift track. Borchetta and Braun are pictured here together.

Image: Kevin Mazur / Getty images

HITTING BACK AT THE MUSIC MOGUL, SHE APPEARED ON THE STAGE WEARING A WHITE SHIRT, WITH THE NAMES OF HER FIRST FIVE ALBUMS ON IT

Fun Fact

TAYLOR MADE A POWERFUL STATEMENT AT THE 2019 AMERICAN MUSIC AWARDS, WHEN SHE TOOK TO THE STAGE TO PERFORM A MEDLEY OF HER BIGGEST HITS. AT THE TIME OF THIS, BRAUN WAS SUPPOSEDLY BLOCKING HER FROM SINGING HER PAST TRACKS AT THE ANNUAL CEREMONY. HITTING BACK AT THE MUSIC MOGUL, SHE APPEARED ON THE STAGE WEARING AN OVERSIZED WHITE SHIRT, WITH THE NAMES OF HER FIRST FIVE ALBUMS EMBLAZONED ACROSS IT. A GROUP OF CHILDREN THEN JOINED TAYLOR ON STAGE, WEARING MATCHING ENSEMBLES THAT FANS SPECULATE IS AN IMPLICATION THAT FUTURE GENERATIONS SHOULD BE ABLE TO OWN THE WORK THEY CREATE.

Image: Emma McIntyre / Getty Images

FEARLESS

The master recordings controversy was not the first time Taylor made a stance about how the music industry operates. In 2014, the singer pulled her music from Spotify, arguing that artists receive a tiny royalty per song play. But she made a return to streaming services in 2017 to thank fans for her album, *1989*, passing ten million sales.

Image: Michelangelo Oprandi / Alamy images

Master recordings regularly change hands, but never hit the headlines, making Taylor's actions even more admirable. She also announced plans to re-record her first five albums, releasing *Fearless (Taylor's Version)* in April 2021 and *RED (Taylor's Version)* in November 2021. At the 2019 Billboard Women in Music Event, she addressed the 'toxic male privilege' of Braun in her acceptance speech for winning the inaugural Woman of the Decade award.

Image: Kevin Mazur / Getty images

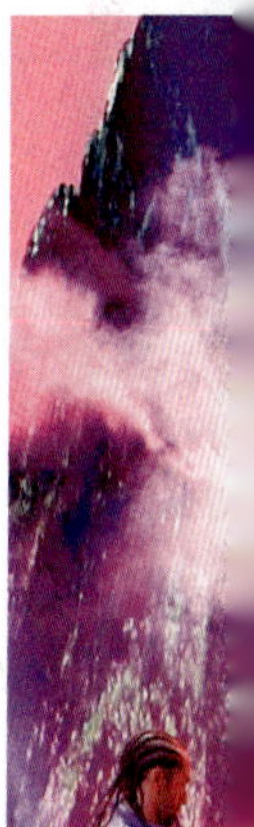

Opening the 2019 Billboard Music Awards with Brendon Urie, Taylor performs 'Me!', the lead single from *Lover* – her first album with new label Republic Records. All about embracing individuality, the song is Taylor's declaration that she has found success in the freedom to be herself – and encourages her fans to do the same.

Image: Ethan Miller / Getty images

Taylor has also spoken out in support of friend and fellow musician, Kesha. The 'Tik Tok' and 'Take It Off 'singer had her own high-profile legal battles to contend with involving her former producer, Dr Luke, who she alleges sexually assaulted her. Among other supporters such as Lady Gaga, Ariana Grande and Miley Cyrus, Taylor posted her support on social media and donated $250,000 to help Kesha with financial needs.

Image: Frazer Harrison /FilmMagic) / Getty images

This rainbow-hued stage production is from Taylor's performance at the 2019 MTV VMAs. At the awards ceremony she won the 'Video of the Year' accolade for 'You Need to Calm Down', a gay anthem in which Taylor voices her support for the LGTBQ+ community. The release of the track resulted in a spike of donations to GLAAD, an organisation battling for LGTBQ+ acceptance, which Taylor namechecked in the lyrics.

Image: Mike Coppola / Getty images

Did you know?

WHEN TAYLOR REVEALED HER LONG-RUNNING STRUGGLE TO RECLAIM HER MUSICAL CATALOGUE, SHE ALSO ENABLED OTHER ARTISTS TO QUESTION THEIR RIGHTS. AFTER WATCHING TAYLOR'S BATTLE PLAY OUT, SINGER-SONGWRITER OLIVIA RODRIGO ANNOUNCED SHE HAD NEGOTIATED WITH HER RECORD LABEL TO OWN HER MASTERS. CANADIAN MUSICIAN BRYAN ADAMS WAS INSPIRED BY TAYLOR TO RE-RECORD HIS OWN BACK CATALOGUE AFTER A DISAGREEMENT WITH HIS RECORD LABEL. JOE JONAS, RITA ORA, SNOOP DOGG AND ASHANTI ARE AMONG THE OTHER ARTISTS WHO HAVE ADMITTED THEY WOULD LIKE TO RE-RECORD THEIR WORK OR PURCHASE THEIR MASTERS FOLLOWING TAYLOR'S EXAMPLE.

Image: Lionel Hahn/ Getty Images

Taylor performed 'The Man' during her one-off City of Lover concert in Paris on 9 September 2019 and the live track was released as a single. In the song, Taylor imagines how she would be treated as a man, calling out double standards, toxic masculinity and the objectification of women. It is an important portrayal of the sexist behaviour women face every day.

Image: Dave Hogan / Getty images

A fan holds up a banner at a Taylor Swift performance in London in 2012 referencing the US elections, despite the singer remaining famously mute on all things politics. But six years later, when Taylor publicly endorsed the Democratic candidate Phil Bredesen for the 2018 senate race, she caused a surge in people registering to vote, an effect the media called the 'Swift Lift'.

Image: Samir Hussein / Getty images

On the opening night of her Eras Tour in Arizona, Taylor entered the stage wearing this bejewelled Versace bodysuit. The first song on the set list was 'Miss Americana and the Heartbreak Prince', a track that Taylor wrote to capture her disillusionment with the state of the American political climate in 2018. It represents one of the singer's first attempts to become more socially engaged.

Image: Kevin Mazur / Getty images

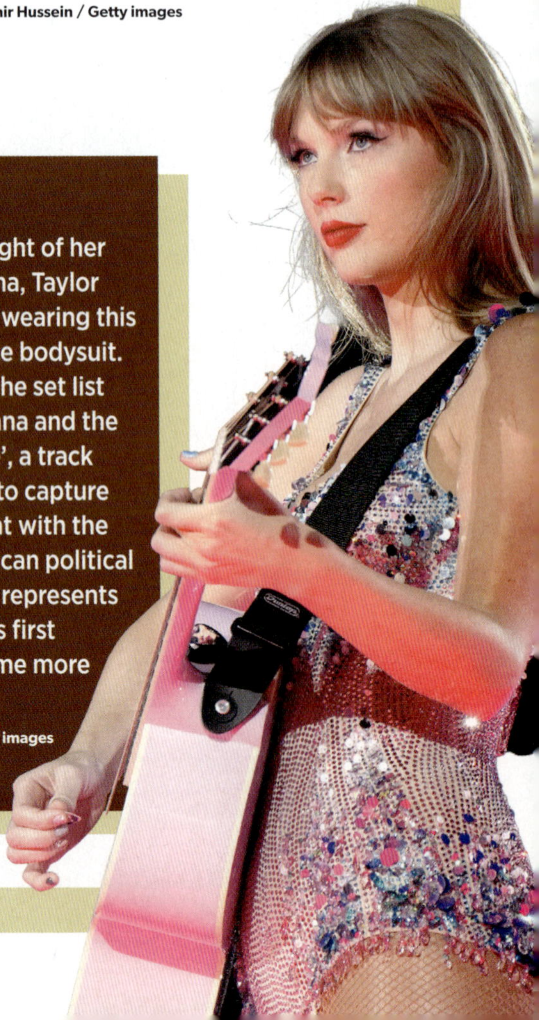

Taylor had a different political game plan for the 2020 US elections. In her Netflix documentary, *Miss Americana*, she expressed regret at not denouncing Donald Trump when he ran for office in 2016. But this time, she posted on Twitter that she would be voting for the Democratic presidential nominee, Joe Biden.

Image: Kevin Dietsch / Getty images

Voting isn't the only area where Taylor has become more vocal. In 2018, she donated to the March for Our Lives rally, a student-led movement against gun violence. Then after the death of George Floyd, who was wrongfully killed by a police officer in May 2020, she used her platform to speak out about the lack of police accountability and the institution's racist behaviour.

Image: David McNew / Getty images

Fun Fact

IF YOU'RE FAMILIAR WITH TAYLOR'S DISCOGRAPHY, YOU MIGHT NOTICE ON EVERY ALBUM THAT TRACK FIVE IS THE MOST HEART-WRENCHING. FROM 'COLD AS YOU' ON HER SELF-TITLED DEBUT TO 'YOU'RE ON YOUR OWN, KID' ON HER 2021 RELEASE *MIDNIGHTS*, THE TRADITION SHOWS TAYLOR IS UNAFRAID TO SHARE HER MOST EMOTIONAL INSIGHTS. "I DIDN'T REALISE I WAS DOING THIS, BUT AS I WAS MAKING ALBUMS, I GUESS I WAS JUST KIND OF PUTTING A VERY VULNERABLE, PERSONAL, HONEST, EMOTIONAL SONG AS TRACK FIVE," SHE ONCE EXPLAINED DURING AN INSTAGRAM LIVE. THE SINGER EVEN WON A GRAMMY AWARD FOR 'WHITE HORSE', WHICH IS TRACK NUMBER FIVE ON THE ALBUM *FEARLESS*.

Image: Robyn Beck / Getty Images

SHE USED HER PLATFORM TO SPEAK OUT ABOUT POLICE ACCOUNTABILITY

LOVER

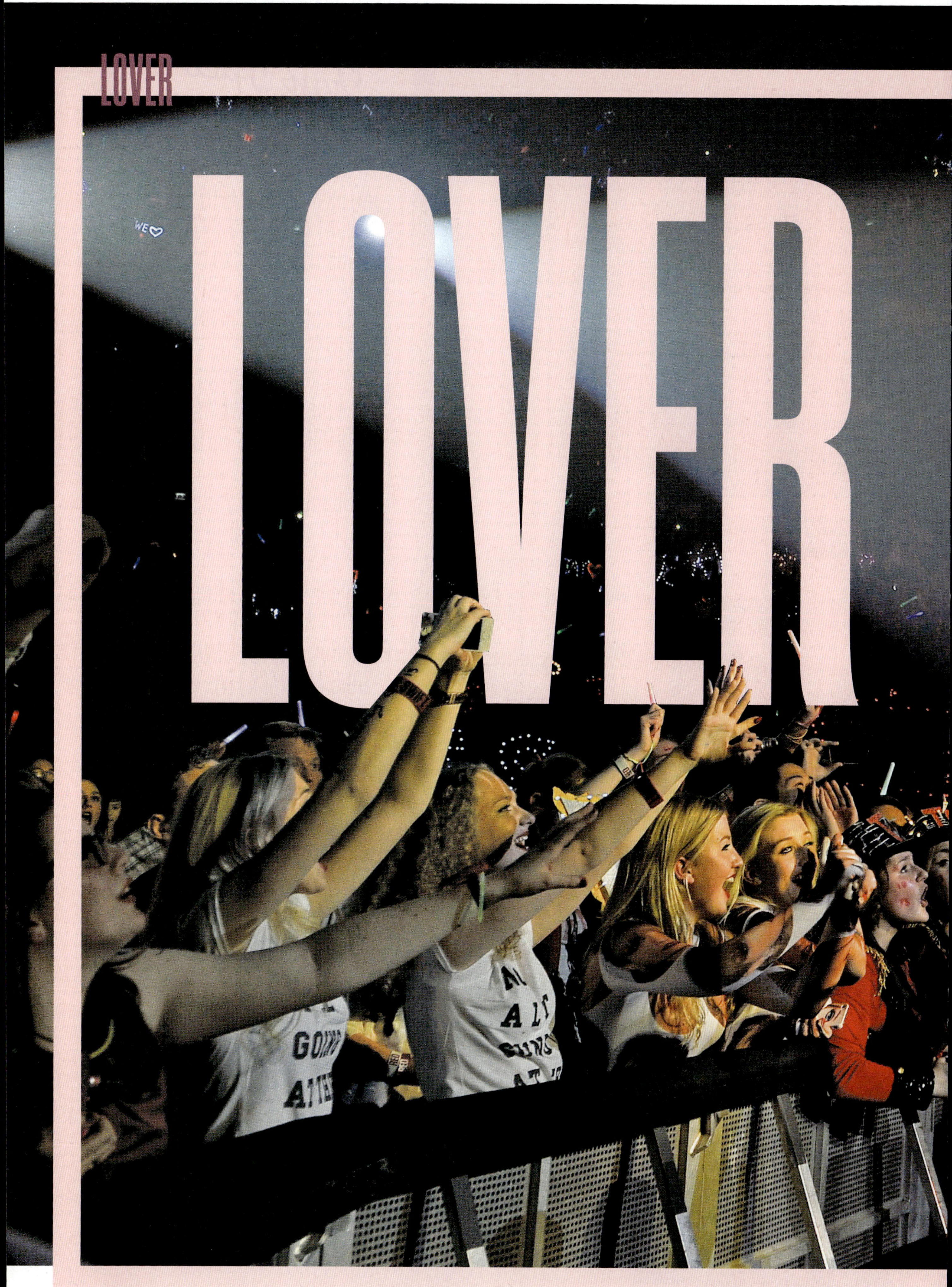

FROM FADED ROMANCES TO A FANDOM UNLIKE ANY OTHER, DISCOVER THE RELATIONSHIPS THAT HAVE SHAPED TAYLOR'S LIFE AND MUSIC

LOVER

Taylor's first high-profile relationship was with Joe Jonas in 2008. But the Jonas Brothers frontman and the 'Love Story' singer only dated for a few months before he broke up with her on a 27-second phone call. Seen here appearing with the band as a guest performer on their Burnin' Up Tour, Taylor was reportedly inspired to write the songs 'Last Kiss' and 'Forever and Always' after the relationship came to its brutal end.

Image: Everett Collection / Disney / Alamy images

When Taylor was 19 years old, she began dating a 31-year-old John Mayer after collaborating with him on his song 'Half of My Heart'. The romance lasted for about four months, but Taylor had enough material to pen the power ballad 'Dear John' – an obvious dig at the singer and how he pursued her despite her young age.

Image: Kevin Mazur / WireImage / Getty images

Affectionately known as Taylor Squared, Taylor Swift and *Twilight* star Taylor Lautner began dating in 2009. The couple met when they co-starred as high school sweethearts in the romantic comedy *Valentine's Day*. Her song 'Back to December', with the lyrics 'Your tanned skin, your sweet smile', is allegedly about the actor and her regret for the way she ended things.

Image: Moviestore Collection / Alamy images

THE LACK OF PRIVACY AND AGE GAP WASN'T WORKING FOR JAKE, SO HE CALLED IT QUITS. LEGEND HAS IT HE STOOD TAYLOR UP ON HER 21ST BIRTHDAY PARTY

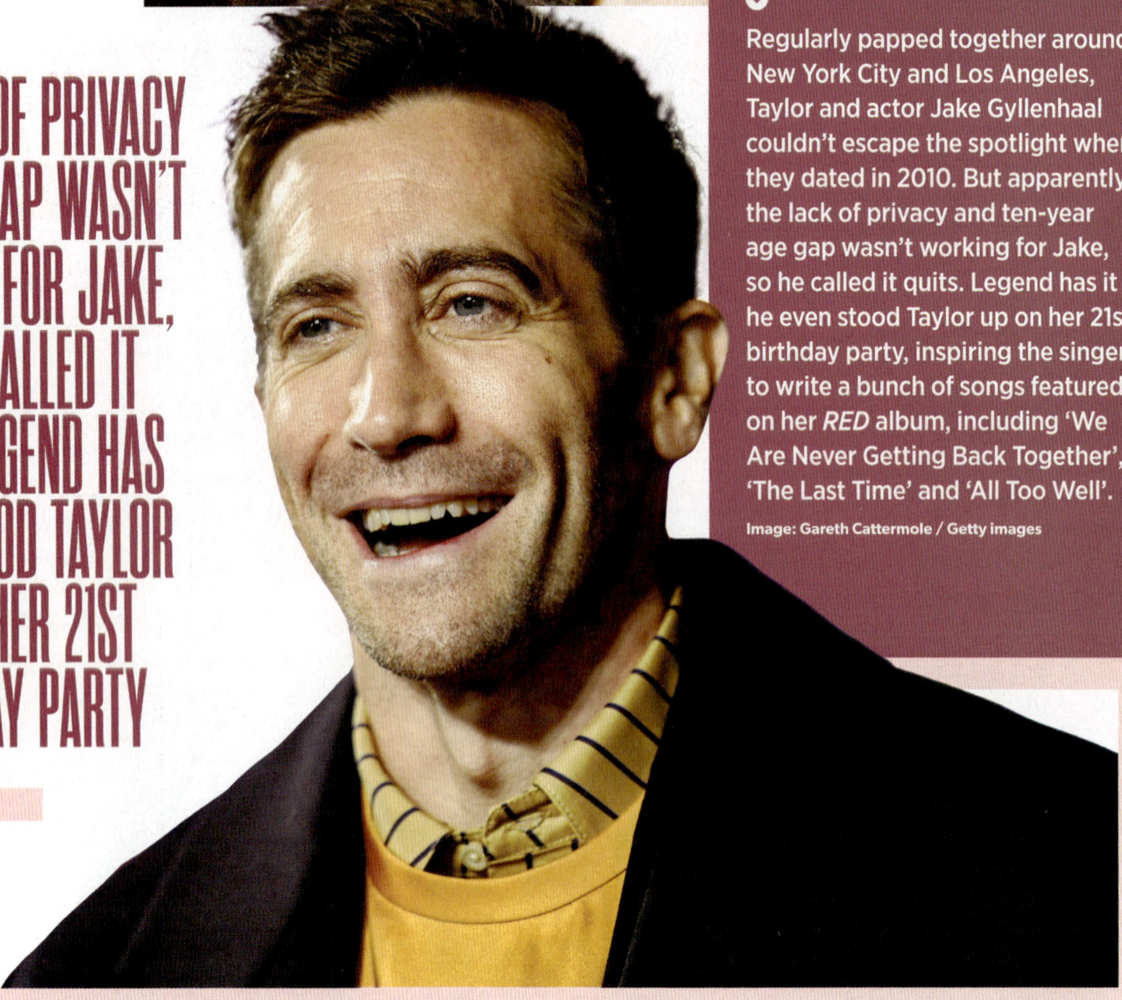

Regularly papped together around New York City and Los Angeles, Taylor and actor Jake Gyllenhaal couldn't escape the spotlight when they dated in 2010. But apparently the lack of privacy and ten-year age gap wasn't working for Jake, so he called it quits. Legend has it he even stood Taylor up on her 21st birthday party, inspiring the singer to write a bunch of songs featured on her *RED* album, including 'We Are Never Getting Back Together', 'The Last Time' and 'All Too Well'.

Image: Gareth Cattermole / Getty images

Harry Styles and Taylor Swift were spotted catching up together at the 2023 Grammy Awards – ten years after a short-lived romance. Despite dating for only three or four months, the couple shared paper aeroplane necklaces, kissed in Times Square on New Year's Eve and even got into a snowmobile accident together. Fans speculate that 'I Knew You Were Trouble' and 'Out of the Woods' were written about the ex-One Direction band member.

Image: Frazer Harrison / Getty images

Mutual friend and fellow singer-songwriter Ellie Goulding introduced Taylor to Scottish DJ Calvin Harris at the Elle Style Awards in 2015. The romance blossomed, with the couple sharing PDAs at music awards, red carpet appearances and adorable Instagram posts. But not long after celebrating their one-year anniversary, the relationship ended abruptly. Some sources say the couple simply weren't compatible, while others claim he was intimidated by her success.

Image: Kevin Winter / Getty images

Not long after Taylor's break up with Calvin Harris, she was spotted kissing British actor Tom Hiddleston on the beach outside her Rhode Island mansion. Their whirlwind romance took them all over the globe, with stops in Tennessee, New York, Australia and England – where the pair were spotted walking along the Norfolk coast with Tom's family. But within a few months, Hiddleswift was no longer a thing.

Image: WENN / Getty images

APPARENTLY, THE SINGER INDULGES IN #TAYLURKING — TRACKING HER OWN FANS ON SOCIAL MEDIA

Did you know?

TOP OF EVERY SWIFTIE'S WISH LIST IS TO BE INVITED TO ONE OF TAYLOR'S SECRET SESSIONS. THESE FAN-ONLY PARTIES BEGAN IN 2014, WHEN TAYLOR REQUESTED THE COMPANY OF SOME OF HER CLOSEST ALLIES SO SHE COULD PLAY THEM HER ALBUM PRIOR TO ITS RELEASE. SINCE THEN, THE GET-TOGETHERS HAVE TAKEN PLACE IN HER VARIOUS HOMES, FROM NEW YORK AND NASHVILLE TO LOS ANGELES, RHODE ISLAND AND LONDON. BUT HOW DOES TAYLOR PICK HER GUESTS? APPARENTLY, THE SINGER INDULGES IN WHAT SHE CALLS #TAYLURKING – TRACKING HER OWN FANS ON SOCIAL MEDIA TO COMPILE THE NEXT GUEST LIST. BUT WHAT HAPPENS IN A SECRET SESSION, STAYS IN A SECRET SESSION.

Image: Mark Metcalfe / Getty Images

LOVER

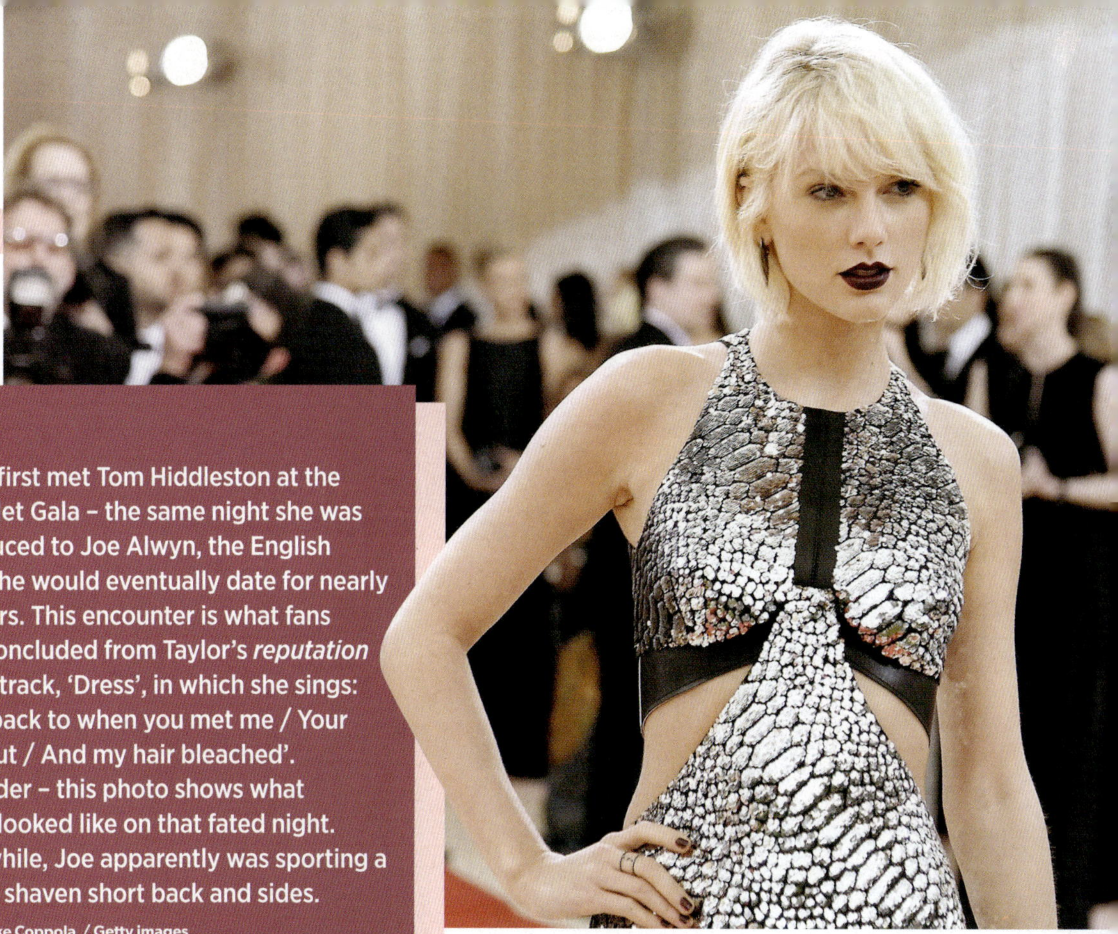

Taylor first met Tom Hiddleston at the 2016 Met Gala – the same night she was introduced to Joe Alwyn, the English actor she would eventually date for nearly six years. This encounter is what fans have concluded from Taylor's *reputation* album track, 'Dress', in which she sings: 'Flashback to when you met me / Your buzz cut / And my hair bleached'. Reminder – this photo shows what Taylor looked like on that fated night. Meanwhile, Joe apparently was sporting a freshly shaven short back and sides.

Image: Mike Coppola / Getty images

News broke in May 2017 – a whole year after the Met Gala – that Taylor was dating Joe. Two years after this, engagement rumours were sparked when Taylor's album, *Lover*, alluded to marriage, but neither party confirmed nor denied the rumours. In fact, compared to previous relationships, Taylor's romance with Joe was kept well out of the public eye.

Image: Christopher Polk / Getty images

Despite keeping her relationship with Joe away from the prying eyes of the press, Taylor still included a variety of subtle and not-so subtle references to the *Conversations with Friends* actor in her music. The track 'London Boy' from *Lover* clearly relates to the actor, as she namechecks city haunts where they've hung out. Joe even collaborated with Taylor on some tracks for her lockdown albums, *folklore* and *evermore* – he's just credited under the pseudonym William Bowery.

Image: Ricky Vigil M / Getty images

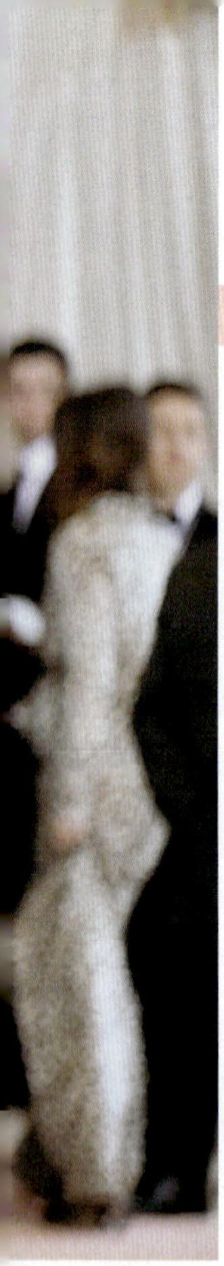

One thing that has been a constant in Taylor's life is her friendship with Abigail Anderson. The BFFs hit it off when they were just 15 years old during their freshman year at Henderson High School in Tennessee. Not only did Abigail inspire the lyrics of Taylor's hit 'Fifteen', but she also appeared in the song's music video. Taylor has even been her best pal's bridesmaid.

Image: Lester Cohen / WireImage / Getty images

Sadly, Taylor's six-year romance with Joe was not meant to be. Reports surfaced in April 2023 that the couple had amicably called it quits. A source told *Entertainment Today* that "the relationship had just run its course". At the time of going to print, Taylor was reportedly dating Matt Healy, the lead vocalist of band the 1975, pictured left.

Image: Emma McIntyre / WireImage / Getty images

ONE CONSTANT IN TAYLOR'S LIFE IS HER FRIENDSHIP WITH ABIGAIL ANDERSON

SELENA GOMEZ AND TAYLOR NOW HAVE ONE OF THE STRONGEST FRIENDSHIPS IN THE MUSIC INDUSTRY

Selena Gomez and Taylor met when they were both dating Jonas brothers in 2008, and now have one of the strongest friendships in the music industry. From hyping each other's music to performing on stage together, they have never stopped publicly supporting one another. Speaking about Taylor in March 2023, Selena said: "She's a role model. I don't think that's something you sign up for; I just think it's something you inherently have inside of you, and I think that's Taylor."

Image: Keven Mazur / Getty images

Did you know?

THE FRIENDSHIP BETWEEN BLAKE LIVELY AND TAYLOR JUST KEEPS GETTING SWEETER. THE BESTIES FIRST MET IN 2014 AND HAVE BEEN HANGING OUT AT PARTIES AND POSTING PICS TOGETHER ON SOCIAL MEDIA EVER SINCE. TAYLOR EVEN SAMPLED BLAKE'S ELDEST DAUGHTER, JAMES, ON HER 2017 SONG 'GORGEOUS'. THEN IN 2020, TAYLOR NAMECHECKED JAMES AND HER TWO YOUNGER SISTERS, INEZ AND BETTY, IN HER SONG 'BETTY' ON HER *FOLKLORE* ALBUM. RECENTLY, BLAKE AND HER HUSBAND RYAN REYNOLDS GAVE UP THEIR LAKESIDE HOME FOR TAYLOR TO USE AS THE SET FOR HER *ALL TOO WELL* SHORT FILM, WHILE THE *GOSSIP GIRL* ACTOR DIRECTED THE MUSIC VIDEO FOR 'I BET YOU THINK ABOUT ME (TAYLOR'S VERSION)' IN 2021.

Image: Theo Wargo / WireImage / Getty Images

The Swift Squad slowly vanished from the public consciousness. An explanation for its disappearance came in 2019, when Taylor wrote an essay for *Elle* magazine in which she mused about outgrowing the friendships she had in her twenties. She also apologised for being so in-your-face-about the girl gang. No names were dropped, but she said how surrounding herself with a clique of friends had come from insecurities she had as a kid about not having any friends. The squad had drawn criticism for being made up of impossibly skinny, mainly white women and for the elitism this entailed.

Image: Kevin Mazur / LP5 / WireImage / Getty images

As Taylor's success skyrocketed, she began to amass more and more celebrity pals. The large yet close-knit circle of friends was dubbed the 'Swift Squad' by the media and included a roll call of in-demand models and actor, including Gigi Hadid, Kendall Jenner, Cara Delevingne, Lily Aldridge, Martha Hunt and Karlie Kloss. During her 1989 Tour, squad members would make surprise appearances on stage and even featured as an ensemble cast in her 2014 single, 'Bad Blood'.

Image: Steve Granitz / WireImage / Getty images

TAYLOR SENT THEM A SATIN PINK BLANKET SHE MADE HERSELF

There was a time when Karlie Kloss and Taylor appeared inseparable. Soon after appearing together at the 2014 Victoria's Secret Fashion Show, the pals solidified their friendship with a well-documented road trip to the Big Sur. Over the years, it appears the pair have drifted apart. While the model asserts they remain good friends, Taylor has stayed silent on the matter. Karlie has been hanging out with Scooter Braun, after all.

Image: Tim P. Whitby / Getty images

Despite the break-up of the Swift Squad, Taylor has remained close to Gigi Hadid. The pair wish each other happy birthday publicly each year, and when Gigi gave birth to a baby girl with her ex-boyfriend Zain Malik, Taylor sent them a satin pink blanket she made herself. The model has even opened up about attending dinner parties hosted by Taylor and claims the singer is an 'exceptional cook'.

Image: Michael Stewart / GC Images / Getty images

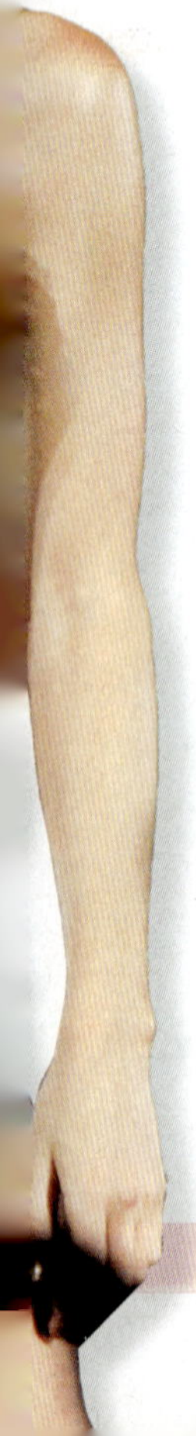

Another friend Taylor shared the stage with during her 1989 World Tour was New Zealand artist Lorde. The 'Royales' singer was taken under Taylor's wing and even appeared in her 'Bad Blood' video. Yet Lorde's close relationship to producer Jack Antonoff allegedly caused a rift between the two friends, especially as Taylor is great pals with Lena Dunham, who was Jack's long-term girlfriend at the time.

Image: Kris Connor / LP5 / Getty images

Fun Fact

TAYLOR JOKED SHE WAS OFFICIALLY THE 'FOURTH HAIM SISTER' AFTER COLLABORATING WITH THE BAND ON A REMIX OF THEIR TRACK 'GASOLINE' IN 2021. BUT THE SINGER'S FRIENDSHIP WITH ALANA, DANIELLE AND ESTE HAIM GOES WAY BACK TO 2014, WITH REPORTS OF SEVEN-HOUR-LONG DINNERS, FOURTH OF JULY PARTIES AND PIZZA-FUELLED SLEEPOVERS TOGETHER. THE BAND EVEN OPENED FOR TAYLOR ON HER 1989 WORLD TOUR AND EIGHT YEARS LATER ON THE ERAS TOUR. IN THE INTERIM, TAYLOR JOINED HAIM ON STAGE AT THE O2 IN LONDON TO PERFORM A MASH UP OF 'LOVE STORY' AND 'GASOLINE', WHERE ALL FOUR MUSICIANS WORE THE SAME BLACK LEATHER TROUSERS (PICTURED HERE). PLUS, 'NO BODY, NO CRIME' ON *EVERMORE* FEATURES GUEST VOCALS FROM HAIM, WITH THE CENTRAL CHARACTER NAMED AFTER ESTE HAIM, AS SHE IS A TRUE CRIME OBSESSIVE.

Image: Nicky J Sims / Getty Images

After meeting at a Golden Globes party in 2014, Taylor and actor, Jaime King, have forged a friendship for life. Taylor was even made a godmother to Jaime's son Leo. Explaining why she picked the singer for the role, the *Hart of Dixie* actor said: "I see what she gives out there to her fans and to her family and that's the kind of person I want to be the guide and the spiritual protector of my child."

Image: Michael Kovac / Getty images

Fun Fact

AROUND 12 MONTHS AFTER BREAKING UP WITH CALVIN HARRIS, TAYLOR WAS UNCOVERED AS CO-WRITER OF HIS SMASH HIT WITH RHIANNA, 'THIS IS WHAT YOU CAME FOR'. AN UNNAMED SOURCE CLAIMS TAYLOR WROTE THE SONG AT HER PIANO BEFORE SENDING AN IPHONE RECORDING TO CALVIN. THE THEN-COUPLE THEN DID A FULL DEMO IN THE STUDIO WITH TAYLOR ON VOCALS AND CALVIN CREATING THE BEATS – THE SAME DEMO LEAKED BY A SUPPOSED HACKER IN MARCH 2023. ON THE FINAL VERSION, TAYLOR'S BACKING VOCALS ARE UNCREDITED, BUT SHE IS CREDITED AS A WRITER, JUST UNDER THE PSEUDONYM OF 'NILS SJÖBERG'.

Image: Kevin Mazur / Getty Images

AFTER BREAKING UP WITH CALVIN HARRIS, TAYLOR WAS UNCOVERED AS CO-WRITER OF HIS SMASH HIT

A friend who goes even further back is actor Emma Stone. She's been tight with Taylor ever since the pair started exchanging emails (yes, it was that long ago!) back in 2009. At one of the pop star's recent Eras Tour concerts, the *Cruella* and *La La Land* actor was spotted in full-on Swiftie mode jamming to 'You Belong to Me' in the VIP section of the arena.

Image: John Shearer / WireImage / Getty images

Despite much internet speculation, Ed Sheeran and Taylor have never dated – they've just been giving us friendship goals since penning the song 'Everything Has Changed' together for Taylor's 2012 album, *RED*. 'The Lego House' singer then opened for Taylor on some RED tour dates, and after gifting each other jam and drinking out of personalised mugs together, the pair duetted again on 'End Game' in 2017 and, most recently, for the remix of Ed's 'The Joker And The Queen'.

Image: Kevin Mazur / WireImage / Getty images

THE BOND TAYLOR SHARES WITH HER FANS HAS EVOLVED INTO SOMETHING MORE LIKE FRIENDSHIP

Ever since the release of her debut album, Taylor has shown her fans a lot of love. From leaving secret messages in album covers to hosting post-show hangouts and marathon meet-and-greets, she has amassed a loyal army of Swifties, whose support only continues to grow.

Image: Dave Hogan / TAS / Getty images

Taylor's generosity knows no bounds when it comes to her fans. She's been reported to surprise Swifties in their own homes, gift huge packages complete with personalised notes, help pay off student loans and deliver Christmas care packages – remember #Swiftmas anyone? Other acts of kindness include regular visits to sick fans in hospital, donating $10,000 for a service dog for a boy with autism and buying a house for a pregnant fan in financial need.

Image: Kevin Mazur / WireImage / Getty images

The bond Taylor shares with her fans has evolved into something more like friendship. This is partly down to the personal and intimate ways she communicates with them, whether it's posting a video on TikTok or broadcasting via Instagram Live. She also comes up with endlessly fascinating ways to keep her fans invested, from hiding Easter eggs in her social media to recruiting Swifties to dance alongside her in the music video for 'Shake It Off'.

Image: Gareth Cattermole / TAS18 / Getty images

Seen here with young ambassadors from Save the Children at Westfield Shopping Centre in London, where she performed a mini-concert, Taylor donates time and funds to charities. She regularly volunteers with the Make-A-Wish Foundation too, while she was moved to write the song 'Ronan' for Maya Thompson, a fan who lost her four-year-old boy Ronan to cancer in 2011.

Image: David M. Benett / Getty images

SHE IS ALWAYS CHAMPIONING LOCAL CAUSES

This photo was taken at Nashville Rising, a benefit concert for flood relief at the Bridgestone Arena in June 2010. Taylor then made a generous donation in the wake of 2017's Hurricane Harvey, followed by $1 million to Nashville tornado relief efforts in March 2020. Always championing local causes, she has also donated $70,000 worth of books to a library in her home state and given money to restore the auditorium of her former high school.

Image: Ed Rode / Getty images

Fun Fact

LENA DUNHAM, THE ACTOR-WRITER-DIRECTOR WHO ROSE TO FAME WITH HER HBO DRAMA *GIRLS*, IS NOW MARRIED TO MUSICIAN LUIS FELBER AND HAD NONE OTHER THAN PAL TAYLOR AS ONE OF HER EIGHT BRIDESMAIDS. THINGS COULD HAVE GOTTEN COMPLICATED FOR THE TWO FRIENDS WHEN LENA BROKE UP WITH TAYLOR'S MUSIC PRODUCER JACK ANTONOFF IN 2018, BUT THEIR BOND HAS PROVED INVINCIBLE. IN FACT, LENA IS ONE OF THE FEW SWIFT SQUAD MEMBERS TO STAND BY AND PUBLICLY SUPPORT THE SINGER IN THE AFTERMATH OF THE KANYE WEST CONTROVERSY – SOMETHING TAYLOR ALLUDED TO IN THE ESSAY SHE WROTE FOR *ELLE* MAGAZINE IN 2019 TO CELEBRATE TURNING 30.

Image: Jeff Kravitz / Getty Images

Did you know?

INTEREST INTO WHAT ACTUALLY WENT ON BETWEEN TAYLOR AND JAKE GYLLENHAAL WAS RECENTLY REIGNITED. IT WAS ALL DOWN TO THE RE-RELEASE OF *RED*, THE ALBUM TAYLOR HAS SINCE CLAIMED IS 'ABOUT A PURE, ABSOLUTE, TO THE CORE HEARTBREAK' WITH THE MARVEL ACTOR BELIEVED TO BE THE SOURCE OF SUCH DISCONTENT. HERE TAYLOR PERFORMS HER NEW VERSION OF 'ALL TOO WELL' ON *SATURDAY NIGHT LIVE* IN NOVEMBER 2021. WHEN ASKED ABOUT HIS THOUGHTS ON THE ALBUM, JAKE GRACIOUSLY REPLIED: "IT HAS NOTHING TO DO WITH ME. IT'S ABOUT HER RELATIONSHIP WITH HER FANS. IT IS HER EXPRESSION. ARTISTS TAP INTO PERSONAL EXPERIENCES FOR INSPIRATION, AND I DON'T BEGRUDGE ANYONE THAT."

Image: Will Heath / NBC / NBCU / Getty Images

While undertaking The Eras Tour in 2023, Taylor made quiet donations to food banks along the way. This generosity was not publicised by the singer, but by the food banks in Arizona and Nevada, which shared the story with local news outlets. Taylor then revealed how she wanted to make a positive impact in the communities where she was touring.

Image: John Shearer / Getty images

TAYLOR REVEALED HOW SHE WANTED TO MAKE A POSITIVE IMPACT IN THE COMMUNITIES WHERE SHE WAS TOURING

Taylor also uses her platform to increase awareness of causes she cares about. Here she performs at Children in Need, helping raise money for disadvantaged kids. Then during the pandemic, she sang at the 'One World: Together at Home' benefit in 2020, as well as making donations to fans who tweeted about the financial struggles they were experiencing due to Covid 19.

Image: PA Images / Getty images

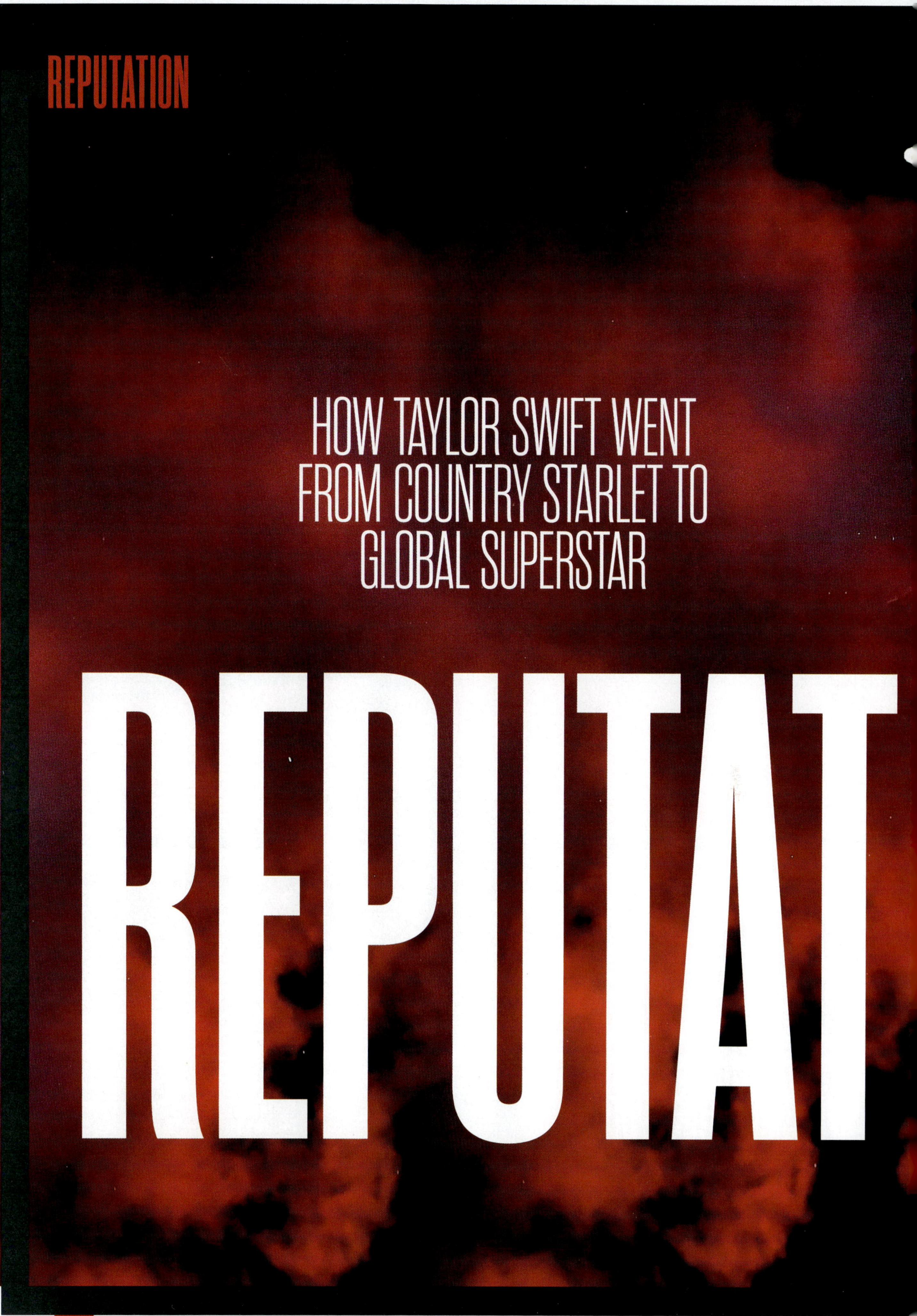

HOW TAYLOR SWIFT WENT FROM COUNTRY STARLET TO GLOBAL SUPERSTAR

REPUTAT

ION

Taylor was just a fresh-faced 16-year-old when she released her self-titled, debut album. Written by the starlet while she was still in high school, the tracks tell the story of a small-town American teenager. But the girl-next-door package proved insanely popular, as Taylor's fresh country sound and autobiographical narratives on romance, friendship and insecurities resonated with audiences across the US and beyond.

Image: Ethan Miller / Getty images

Embarking on a six-month radio tour, Taylor worked tirelessly to promote her first album after it was released in 2006. As her reputation grew, she even got to open for some big country names she admired, including Brad Paisley, Kenny Chesney, and Tim McGraw and Faith Hill. The young singer would then go on to perform alongside her idols later in her career. She's pictured on stage here with Faith Hill in 2010.

Image: Frederick Breedon / WireImage / Getty images

Fun Fact

SWIFTIES SINCE THE BEGINNING WILL KNOW TAYLOR INCLUDED HIDDEN MESSAGES IN THE CD LINERS OF HER FIRST FIVE ALBUMS. SEEMINGLY RANDOM CAPITAL LETTERS IN THE LYRIC BOOKLETS WHEN PUT TOGETHER SPELL OUT PHRASES THAT PROVIDE CLUES FOR THE SUBJECT OF EVERY SONG. FOR EXAMPLE, IN THE LYRIC SHEET FOR *FEARLESS*, TAYLOR CAPITALISED LETTERS THAT SPELT OUT 'I CRIED WHILE RECORDING THIS' FOR THE SONG 'FIFTEEN'. FOR THE HIT SONG '22' ON HER ALBUM *RED*, THE CAPITAL LETTERS SPELL OUT 'ASHLEY DIANNA CLAIRE SELENA', A REFERENCE TO HER BFFS AT THE TIME. MESSAGES ON *1989* INCLUDE 'SHE DANCED TO FORGET HIM' FOR 'SHAKE IT OFF' AND 'SHE MADE FRIENDS AND ENEMIES' FOR 'BAD BLOOD'.

Image: Kevin Mazur / TCA / Getty Images

FEARLESS HAD MAJOR CROSSOVER APPEAL, CATAPULTING TAYLOR INTO THE MAINSTREAM

When Taylor's second album, *Fearless*, arrived in November 2008, she had already reached headliner status. Starting her first ever concert tour in Indiana in April 2009, she performed across North America, Europe, Australia and Asia. Following on from its predecessor, *Fearless* had major crossover appeal, catapulting Taylor out of the country charts and into the mainstream.

Image: Jason Kempin / Getty images

Having written or co-written all the album tracks on *Fearless*, Taylor brought in fairy-tale imagery, such as princesses, princes and white horses, to explore falling in love and starry-eyed romances. The lead single, 'Love Story', is about a troubled romance ending in a marriage proposal with references to Shakespeare's *Romeo and Juliet*, hence the red, Elizabethan-style dress she wore while performing the track on tour.

Image: Jason Kempin / Getty images

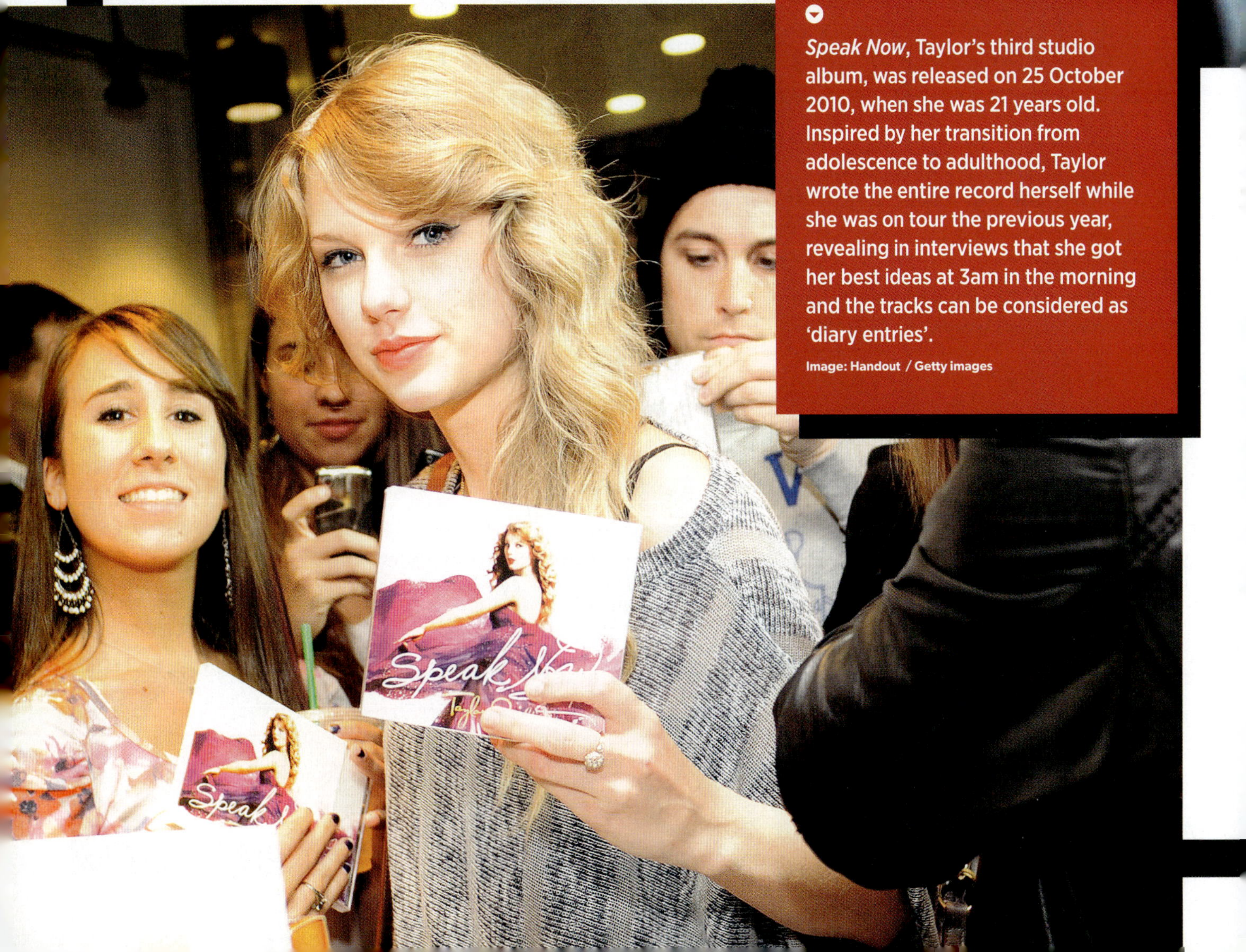

***Speak Now*, Taylor's third studio album, was released on 25 October 2010, when she was 21 years old. Inspired by her transition from adolescence to adulthood, Taylor wrote the entire record herself while she was on tour the previous year, revealing in interviews that she got her best ideas at 3am in the morning and the tracks can be considered as 'diary entries'.**

Image: Handout / Getty images

Love and heartache are still very much central themes in Taylor's third album, but a few songs explore her new experiences of being in the public eye. Now known for her trademark blend of country and pop, she began the Speak Now World Tour in early 2011, performing in stadiums for the very first time. Here she's seen performing at the LG Arena in Birmingham, England.

Image: Dave Hogan / Getty images

LOVE AND HEARTACHE ARE STILL VERY MUCH CENTRAL THEMES TO TAYLOR'S THIRD ALBUM

Not only did *Fearless* bring Taylor legions of new fans and commercial success, it also wowed music industry insiders. Selling 3.217 million copies in the US alone in 2009, the album won Grammys for the Best Country Album and Album of the Year, making Taylor, who was 20 at the time, the youngest artist to ever win the award.

Image: Kevin Winter / Getty images

Taylor's fourth album, *RED*, moves away from the fantasy-driven narratives and happy endings of her previous work. Released in autumn 2012, the record faces up to the stark reality that love can sometimes come to a messy, painful end, with the title referring to the tumultuous 'red' emotions she felt during the album's conception, evoked by unhealthy romantic relationships.

Image: Larry Bussaca / Getty images

Iconic imagery from the RED Tour will forever be associated with her hits from the album, 'We Are Never Ever Getting Back Together' and 'I Knew You Were Trouble'. Laying bare her emotional life, she was beginning to outgrow her public image of an innocent sweetheart, as well as contemplate themes such as one's perceived image and the pressures of fame.

Image: Nicky Loh / Getty images

Did you know?

BEFORE EVERY SHOW ON THE AMERICAN AND AUSTRALIAN LEGS OF HER SPEAK NOW WORLD TOUR, TAYLOR WOULD WRITE SONG LYRICS ON HER LEFT ARM WITH A BLACK SHARPIE. BUT THEY WEREN'T LYRICS OF HER OWN CREATION. INSTEAD, THE INSPIRING LINES WERE TAKEN FROM SONGS THAT SPOKE TO HER FROM DIFFERENT ARTISTS, RANGING FROM FELLOW COUNTRY STARS FAITH HILL AND THE DIXIE CHICKS TO ROCKERS U2 AND TOM PETTY. SHE EVEN PENNED LINES FROM BEST FRIEND SELENA GOMEZ'S HITS 'WHO SAYS' AND 'GHOST OF YOU'. TAYLOR TOLD FANS THE WORDS SHOULD BE VIEWED AS A NIGHTLY 'MOOD RING' AS SHE PICKED THE SONG DEPENDING ON HOW SHE FELT THAT DAY.

Image: Larry Busacca / Getty Images

The RED Tour made history when it grossed $150 million – the highest amount ever for a county artist. But Taylor was making a gradual transition to pop, with *RED* showcasing a range of musical styles Taylor called a 'metaphor for how messy a real break up is'. It required the star to venture outside of her comfort zone by collaborating with new producers and other musicians – such as Ed Sheeran who provided guest vocals on the track 'Everything Has Changed'.

Image: Gareth Cattermole / TAS / Getty images

Following the pop- and electronic-influenced *RED*, Taylor's status as a country musician was already being questioned. But the release of the singer's *1989* album in October 2014 well and truly cemented her status as a pop star. The name of this fifth album, which is Taylor's year of birth, signifies her symbolic re-birth as she worked with renowned pop producers Max Martin and Shellback, and brought a fiercer look to her stage shows.

Image: Christopher Polk / Getty images

THE RELEASE OF THE SINGER'S 1989 ALBUM IN OCTOBER 2014 WELL AND TRULY CEMENTED HER STATUS AS A POP STAR

Expanding on her songwriting skills, Taylor took inspiration from her personal life for the tracks on *RED*. Unlike previous albums, she did not villainise past lovers but wrote from a perspective. Coming under scrutiny from the tabloids, she also used the album as an opportunity to satirise the media's perception of her as a serial dater in songs such as 'Blank Space' and 'Shake It Off' – which won Song of the Year at the iHeartRadio Music Awards in 2015.

Image: Kevin Mazur / Getty images

The 1989 World Tour became the highest grossing tour in 2015, with critics praising the production and Taylor's mesmerising stage presence. Her performances will also be remembered for the appearances of unannounced special guests, which included a roll call of her celeb friends including the likes of Cara Delevingne, Kendall Jenner, Karlie Kloss, Martha Hunt and Gigi Hadid.

Image: Brian Rasic / LP5 / Getty images

After her 1989 World Tour, Taylor disappeared from the public eye to avoid the media's increasing scrutiny and frenzy about her private life and the infamous fall out between the singer and Kanye West. Taking a bigger break than normal between records, she was back in the autumn of 2017 with her sixth studio album, *reputation*. The star refused to speak to the press, but drag racer Courtney Force competed on track with the album imagery plastered on her Chevrolet Camaro.

Image: David Becker / Getty images

Fun Fact

LEAVING SECRET MESSAGES IN THE CD LINERS OF HER ALBUMS WAS JUST THE BEGINNING FOR TAYLOR. FOR OVER A DECADE NOW, SHE'S BECOME A MASTER AT DROPPING CRYPTIC CLUES AND HIDDEN MESSAGES FOR HER FANS TO DECIPHER AND ADMITS SHE "LOVES TO COMMUNICATE THROUGH EASTER EGGS". DURING HER *REPUTATION* ERA, THIS INVOLVED PLANTING 'THOUSANDS' OF VISUAL EASTER EGGS INTO THE VIDEO FOR 'LOOK WHAT YOU MADE ME DO', NODDING TO HER RIVALS AND PAST SCANDALS. WHILE THE MUSIC VIDEO FOR 2019 SINGLE 'ME!' FEATURING BRENDON URIE OF PANIC! AT THE DISCO (SEEN PERFORMING TOGETHER HERE) HINTED AT HER NEXT ALBUM'S TITLE – YOU CAN SEE THE WORDS 'LOVER' APPEAR AT THE 1.56 TIMESTAMP IN THE VIDEO.

Image: Kevin Winter / Getty Images

Just before *reputation's* launch, Taylor generated a huge amount of speculation by clearing her website and social media accounts of content. The hype paid off as fans were introduced to a darker side of the singer. Not only is the electropop sound of the album far heavier than her previously bright and breezy tracks, but the lyrics also deal with grittier topics such as vengeance, the downside of fame and the resultant anger.

Image: Alexander Tamargo / Getty images

FOR OVER A DECADE NOW, SHE'S BECOME A MASTER AT DROPPING CRYPTIC CLUES AND HIDDEN MESSAGES

REPUTATION

Taylor would reinvent herself again with the release of her seventh studio album, *Lover*. Pictured here introducing the record in Brooklyn, New York, Taylor unleashed a newfound creativity to write the tracks after recalibrating her personal life and freeing herself from her public image. As a result, the record features bright, light-hearted vibes with confessional and playful songs about love and emotional intimacy.

Image: Gotham / Getty images

Taylor told *Rolling Stone* in 2019 that she conceptualised *Lover* as "just a barn wood floor and some ripped curtains flowing in the breeze, and fields of flowers". Unfortunately Covid-19 scuppered her touring plans, so fans didn't see how her seventh album would be brought to life. But tracks from the album featured in the set list of her 2023 Eras Tour, pictured here.

Image: Omar Vega / TAS23 / Getty images

Taylor told *Rolling Stone* that she conceptualised *reputation* as a "night-time cityscape" with "old warehouse buildings that had been deserted". This, together with the themes of the album, were in the stage production for the reputation Stadium Tour, pictured here. Incorporating goth subculture, snake motifs and Broadway theatricality, it became the highest ever grossing tour in North America by a female artist.

Image: Don Arnold / Getty images

Swifties were ecstatic when Taylor released a surprise album in July 2020 called *folklore*, which went on to win a Grammy for Album of the Year. On stage with Taylor are producers Jack Antonoff and Aaron Dessner, who she worked with virtually – due to the Covid-19 quarantine measures – to record the album. In Taylor's own words, *folklore* is "a collection of songs and stories that flowed like a stream of consciousness".

Image: Kevin Winter / Getty images

TAYLOR UNLEASHED A NEWFOUND CREATIVITY TO WRITE THE TRACKS

Lover won the Favourite Album award at the 2019 American Music Awards and became the best selling global album of the year by a solo artist. Most of the tracks were recorded in New York with Taylor's long-term collaborator Jack Antonoff, whose production is characterised by 1980s drums, atmospheric synthesisers, and reverbed beats. The vocals were recorded as if Taylor was performing live, with the majority of the tracks said to be full takes.

Image: JC Olivera / Getty images

REPUTATION

Taylor treated audiences at the 2021 Grammy Awards to an acoustic performance of three tracks from *folklore*. Departing from the upbeat pop of Taylor's previous albums, *folklore* features mellow ballads, taking inspiration from indie folk, alternative rock and electroacoustic styles. Exploring escapism, empathy and nostalgia, the record also diverts from the singer's back catalogue by swapping autobiographical details for a new rota of characters and story arcs.

Image: TAS Rights Management 2021 / Getty images

THE RECORD SWAPS AUTOBIOGRAPHICAL DETAILS FOR NEW CHARACTERS AND STORY ARCS

Did you know?

TAYLOR WENT IN HEAVY WITH THE SNAKE IMAGERY DURING HER REPUTATION TOUR. FROM A MECHANISED COBRA TO SNAKE MERCHANDISE, SNAKE-EMBROIDERED CLOTHING AND A SNAKE MICROPHONE, THE REPTILIAN CREATURE WAS EVERYWHERE. IT WAS PART OF TAYLOR'S PLOY TO RECLAIM THE MOTIF AFTER BEING CALLED A SNAKE BY KIM KARDASHIAN, FOLLOWING A FEUD WITH THE REALITY TV STAR AND HER THEN HUSBAND, KANYE WEST. AFTER BEING HOUNDED BY SOCIAL MEDIA USERS WITH THE SNAKE EMOJI, THE REPUTATION TOUR WAS TAYLOR'S STAND AGAINST THE ONLINE BULLIES. OF THE SITUATION, SHE SAID: "I LEARNED A REALLY IMPORTANT LESSON THAT I'VE BEEN TELLING YOU FROM THE STAGE FOR ABOUT TEN YEARS, BUT I NEVER HAD TO LEARN IT SO HARSHLY MYSELF – AND THAT LESSON HAS TO DO WITH HOW MUCH YOU VALUE YOUR REPUTATION."

Image: Don Arnold / TAS18 / Getty Images

Another surprise album, *evermore*, arrived in December 2020 five months after *folklore*. Both lockdown albums are said to be sister projects, but Taylor explained in an Apple Music interview that while *folklore* deals with "conflict resolution", *evermore* explores "endings of all sorts, sizes and shapes" and the pain and phases of such closures. Combining indie folk with chamber pop styles, Taylor again wowed fans worldwide.

Image: Mark Metcalfe / Getty images

In *Midnights*, Taylor returns to her first-person storytelling. Calling it a story of "13 sleepless nights scattered throughout my life", the album abounds with confessional yet cryptic lyrics, exploring themes such as self-hatred, revenge fantasies, wondering what might have been, falling in love and falling apart. Expanding on the synth-pop of her previous albums, the songs experiment with subtle grooves, vintage synthesisers and chill-out music.

Image: Mike Kemp / Getty images

Taylor announced the release of her tenth studio album, *Midnights* – at midnight. It followed the 2022 MTV VMA, where she wore a navy blue Moschino dress embroidered with silver stars to an after party, subtly hinting at the name of her fifth album in three years. It went on to become the singer's most commercially successful album.

Image: Gotham / Getty images

In April 2022, Taylor released a re-recording of her second studio album, with the title *Fearless (Taylor's version)*. Although the album was praised by critics and fans alike, it was not created under the best of circumstances, as it followed a dispute over the ownership of the masters to Taylor's first six studio albums. The promotional campaign included a prime billboard spot in New York's Times Square.

Image: Noam Galai / Getty images

POP CULTURE
MARRIOTT MARQUIS
YOU'LL NEVER GUESS WHO.
THE MASKED SINGER
amazon music
ALEXA, OPEN
TAYLOR'S VERSION
AMERICAN EAGLE OUTFITTERS
STARRING GRAMMY
THROUGH NOV 24 ONLY!
THE HIT BR
BARRYMORE THEATRE
LARGEST, FAS
MOST RELIABLE

Seven months later, Taylor released the second of her re-recorded albums, *RED (Taylor's Version)*, as part of her countermeasure against the purchase of her back catalogue. The album's 30 tracks are made up of 20 from the deluxe edition of RED, as well as previously unreleased 'from-the-vault' offerings. Ed Sheeran and Gary Lightbody even returned to provide guest vocals, and it racked up even more awards and accolades, such as Favourite Pop Album at the 2022 American Music Awards.

Image: Matt Winkelmeyer / Getty images

After the Covid-19 pandemic put a halt to Taylor's Lover Tour, she decided to change the focus of her stadium visits in 2023. Called the Eras Tour, the 44-song set list took concert-goers on a journey through Taylor's musical eras, serving as a reminder of how Taylor began as a Nashville country starlet and rose to become a musical superstar, overcoming intense media scrutiny about her personal life, public fallouts and feuds, and music ownership controversy along the way.

Image: Ethan Miller /TAS23 / Getty images

Fun Fact

ALTHOUGH UNLUCKY FOR SOME, THE NUMBER 13 IS TAYLOR'S FAVOURITE – SHE EVEN WENT THROUGH A PHRASE OF DRAWING IT ONTO HER HAND (SOMETIMES IN EYELINER) BEFORE HER BIG STAGE PERFORMANCES. WHEN INTERVIEWED ABOUT THE SIGNIFICANCE OF THE NUMBER, THE CONNECTIONS TURNED OUT TO BE UNCANNY. NOT ONLY IS TAYLOR BORN ON 13 DECEMBER, SHE TURNED 13 ON FRIDAY 13TH, HER FIRST ALBUM WENT GOLD IN 13 WEEKS AND HER FIRST NUMBER-ONE SONG HAD A 13-SECOND INTRO. "BASICALLY WHENEVER A 13 COMES UP IN MY LIFE, IT'S A GOOD THING," SHE SAID IN A 2009 MTV INTERVIEW. IN A NOD TO HER LUCKY NUMBER, THE DIGITS OF *LOVER*, *FOLKLORE*, AND *MIDNIGHTS* ALBUM RELEASE DATES ALSO EACH ADD UP TO 13.

Image: Fred Duval / Film Magic / Getty Images

THE NUMBER 13 IS TAYLOR'S FAVOURITE — SHE WENT THROUGH A PHRASE OF DRAWING IT ONTO HER HAND

FOLKLORE

BREAKING RECORDS AT EVERY TURN, TAYLOR'S METEORIC CULTURAL IMPACT WILL LONG GO DOWN IN HISTORY

A shocked-looking Taylor picks up the award for Entertainer of the Year at the Annual Country Music Association Awards in 2009. Just 19 at the time, she was the youngest ever country star to receive the accolade, but she was breaking records way earlier than this. In 2006, after the release of 'Our Song', she became the youngest artist in history to have written and performed a number one song on the Hot Country Songs chart.

Image: Rick Diamond / Getty images

Both rising to fame in the late noughties, it's no surprise Taylor became friends with Miley Cyrus – she even had a cameo in *Hannah Montana: The Movie*. Here the pals perform 'Fifteen' together at the 2009 Grammy Awards. Fast forward one year and Taylor scooped the Grammy for Album of the Year for *Fearless*, making her the youngest artist at the time to triumph in the category.

Image: Kevin Mazur / Getty images

Since winning her first Grammy Award, Taylor has tallied up 12 in total and gone on to set even more records. She is the first and only woman to win thrice – that's three times – in the prestigious Album of the Year category, with Fearless (2009), *1989* (2016) and *Folklore* (2021), and is the female artist with the most nominations for Song of the Year, despite never winning the accolade.

Image: Jay L. Clendenin / Los Angeles Times / Getty images

SINCE WINNING HER FIRST GRAMMY, TAYLOR HAS TALLIED UP 12 IN TOTAL

Fun Fact

TAYLOR CAN ALSO ADD AWARD-WINNING FILMMAKER TO HER JAM-PACKED RESUME. IN 2021, SHE WROTE AND DIRECTED *ALL TOO WELL: THE SHORT FILM* – A 14-MINUTE VIDEO STARRING SADIE SINK AND DYLAN O'BRIEN AS THE YOUNG LOVERS WHOSE ILL-FATED RELATIONSHIP IS CHRONICLED IN THE LYRICS OF THE 2012 POWER BALLAD. THE SINGER-TURNED-FILMMAKER THEN SCOOPED THREE AWARDS FOR THE FILM AT THE 2022 MTV VIDEO MUSIC AWARDS, INCLUDING BEST DIRECTION, BEST LONGFORM VIDEO AND THE HIGHLY COVETED VIDEO OF THE YEAR. THIS HAS MADE TAYLOR THE FIRST ARTIST EVER TO WIN VIDEO OF THE YEAR THREE TIMES, AND THE FIRST ARTIST IN HISTORY TO WIN VIDEO OF THE YEAR FOR A SELF-DIRECTED VIDEO.

Image: Dimitrios Kambouris / Getty Images

- While Taylor can't quite match Beyonce's 32 Grammys, the 'Anti-Hero' singer has a mammoth 40 American Music Awards to her name. She dominated the 2022 ceremony, taking home all six awards she was nominated for. This haul makes her the artist with the most wins at the annual awards, easily eclipsing second-ranked Michael Jackson with his 26 trophies.

Image: Tommaso Boddi / WireImage / Getty images

Looking glam in black sequins, Taylor performs at the Nashville Songwriters Awards in 2022, before being named the Songwriter-Artist of the Decade. Her set included 'All Too Well (10-minute version)', a song she re-recorded for *RED (Taylor's Version)* and which is now the longest single in history to reach number one in the Billboard Hot 100.

Image: Terry Wyatt / Getty images

- Walking the red carpet at the 2022 MTV Video Music Awards (VMAs), Taylor is certainly no stranger to coming out on top at this star-studded event. In 2022 alone, she picked up four awards, making her the only artist to have ever won the highly coveted video of the year award three times – for 'Bad Blood' (2015), 'You Need to Calm Down' (2019) and 'All Too Well' (2022).

Image: Arturo Holmes/FilmMagic / Getty images

IN 2022, SHE PICKED UP FOUR MTV AWARDS, MAKING HER THE ONLY ARTIST TO HAVE EVER WON THE VIDEO OF THE YEAR AWARD THREE TMES

For many, the most memorable MTV VMAs moment involving Taylor was in 2009 when Kanye West interrupted her on stage mid-acceptance speech. But she's also put on some iconic performances, like at the 2015 ceremony when she joined Nicki Minaj on stage for a mash-up of 'The Night is Still Young' and 'Bad Blood', stomping out rumours of a supposed feud between the two singers.

Image: John Shearer / Getty images

FOLKLORE

The silverware in Taylor's trophy cabinet doesn't just reflect her talent as a singer-songwriter. In December 2011, she was bestowed with the Harmony Award at the Nashville Symphony Ball, which paid tribute to how she reflects the unique harmony between the many worlds of music that exist in Nashville.

Image: Royce DeGrie / Getty images

At the 2019 American Music Awards, Taylor received the first ever Artist of the Decade award. To celebrate this honour, she performed a medley of her best tracks, which culminated in 'Lover' with the singer adorned in a bubble-gum pink cape. During her acceptance speech, the singer said the honour celebrated ten years of "hard work and of art and of fun and memories".

Image: Emma McIntyre/AMA2019 / Getty images

Taylor might have left school at 17 to pursue a career in music, but in 2022 she received an honorary doctorate in fine arts from New York University. At the ceremony in the city's iconic Yankee Stadium, she gave a rousing speech to graduates advising them to follow their 'gut instincts' even in the face of fear.

Image: Angela Weiss / AFP / Getty images

Dressed in a statement bejewelled jumpsuit at the 2023 iHeartRadio Music Awards, Taylor took home the Song of the Year award for 'Anti-Hero'. The track is taken from her album *Midnights*, which made Spotify history when it was released on 1 October 2022 by becoming the most streamed album on a single day. With 184 million streams, it beat the previous record of 153 million streams set by Drake's *Certified Lover Boy*.

Image: Jeff Kravitz / Getty images

TAYLOR WAS PRESENTED WITH THE BRIT'S GLOBAL ICON AWARD IN 2021 TO RECOGNISE HER IMMENSE IMPACT ON MUSIC AROUND THE WORLD

Did you know?

WHEN TAYLOR RELEASED HER ALBUM *FOLKLORE* IN JULY 2020, IT SPARKED A MAJOR BUZZ AROUND THE TERM 'FOLKLORE'. IN RESPONSE TO A GIGANTIC INFLUX OF INTERNET USERS SEARCHING FOR THE WORD'S DEFINITION, THE AMERICAN FOLKLORE SOCIETY LAUNCHED A NEW WEBSITE TITLED 'WHAT IS FOLKLORE?', WHILE FOLKLORISTS WERE RECRUITED TO HELP PROMOTE THE ACADEMIC FIELD ON SOCIAL MEDIA. THE SINGER HERSELF WEIGHED IN ON THE DISCUSSION WITH THIS INSIGHT: "A TALE THAT BECOMES FOLKLORE IS ONE THAT IS PASSED DOWN AND WHISPERED AROUND. SOMETIMES EVEN SUNG ABOUT. THE LINES BETWEEN FANTASY AND REALITY BLUR AND BOUNDARIES BETWEEN TRUTH AND FICTION BECOME ALMOST INDISCERNIBLE."

Image: Octavio Jones / TAS23 / Getty Images

Loved and adored by fans on all continents, Taylor was presented with the BRIT's Global Icon Award in 2021 to recognise her immense impact on music around the world. She is the first ever female recipient of the award, which is reserved for truly exceptional artists. Previous winners include British music legends Elton John, David Bowie and Robbie Williams.

Image: Dave J Hogan / Getty images

We all know Taylor is an icon, but she has the awards to prove it. In 2019, she received the inaugural Teen Icon Award at the Teen Choice Awards dressed in a colourful Versace shorts co-ord. She has won more Teen Choice Awards than any other artist in history and used the moment in 2019 to address gender pay inequality and remind young fans that mistakes are inevitable.

Image: FOX Image Collection Getty images

Another feat only Taylor has achieved is taking over the entire top ten of the Billboard Hot 100 chart. The never-seen-before moment happened when the singer released *Midnights*, with her single 'Anti-Hero' taking the number-one spot. Here Taylor is celebrating at the Billboard Music Awards in 2019 with Panic! At The Disco's Brendon Urie.

Image: Ethan Miller / Getty images

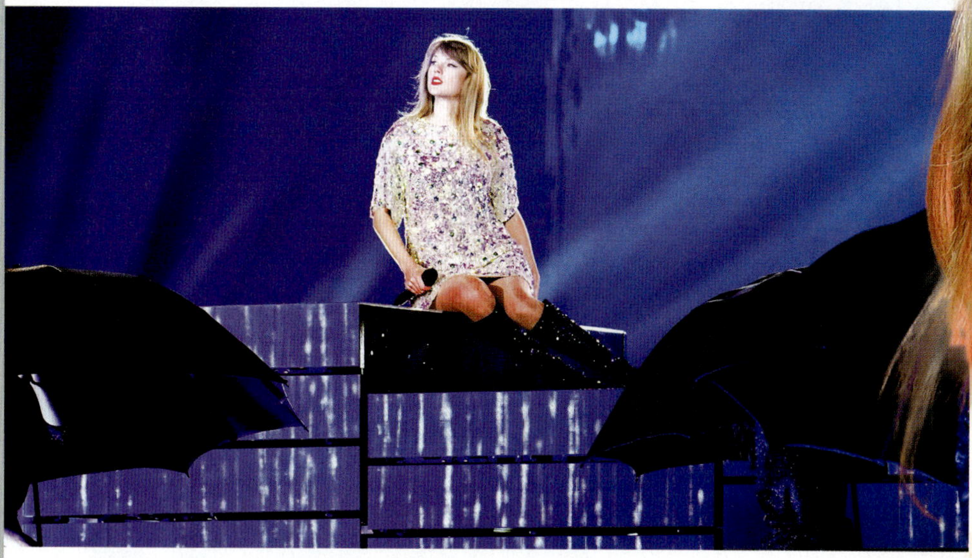

During her 2023 Eras Tour, Taylor performed tracks from her 2022 album *Midnights* in a glittering Oscar de la Renta t-shirt. It's definitely an unforgettable era for Taylor as she once again proved her unmatched popularity, selling more than a record-breaking six million albums in less than eight weeks. The album also became the highest-selling vinyl album of the 21st century.

Image: Kevin Mazur / Getty images

The 1989 World Tour became the highest grossing tour in 2015, with critics praising the production and Taylor's mesmerising stage presence. Her performances will also be remembered for the appearances of unannounced special guests, which included a roll call of her celeb friends including the likes of Cara Delevingne, Kendall Jenner, Karlie Kloss, Martha Hunt and Gigi Hadid.

Image: Angela Weiss / Frazer Harrison / Getty images

Fun Fact

SWIFTIES REJOICE, YOU CAN NOW STUDY TAYLOR SWIFT AT UNIVERSITY – AND THERE'S MORE THAN ONE COURSE AVAILABLE. THE POP STAR FIRST BECAME THE SUBJECT OF AN UNDERGRADUATE COURSE IN 2022 WHEN NEW YORK UNIVERSITY'S CLIVE DAVIS INSTITUTE LAUNCHED A CLASS COVERING SWIFT'S EVOLUTION AS A CREATIVE MUSIC ENTREPRENEUR. TEXAS UNIVERSITY FOLLOWED A FEW MONTHS LATER BY OFFERING A COURSE TITLED 'THE TAYLOR SWIFT SONGBOOK' WHILE THE LATEST INSTITUTION TO GET IN ON THE ACTION IS STANFORD UNIVERSITY, WITH ITS TEN-WEEK COURSE PROMISING AN IN-DEPTH ANALYSIS OF THE SONG 'ALL TOO WELL (10-MINUTE VERSION)'. THERE'S EVEN A SUMMER SCHOOL CLASS AVAILABLE IN THE UK AT THE QUEEN MARY UNIVERSITY OF LONDON, WHICH PROMPTS STUDENTS TO EXPLORE THE QUESTION 'IS THE WORK OF TAYLOR SWIFT LITERATURE?'.

Image: Dia Dipasupil / Getty Images

Did you know?

TICKETS TO THE ERAS TOUR WERE IN SUCH HIGH DEMAND THE TICKETMASTER WEBSITE CRASHED ON THE FIRST DAY OF PRESALE. NEVER BEFORE HAD THE COMPANY EXPERIENCED THE SHEER FORCE OF HUNDREDS OF THOUSANDS OF SWIFTIES, AS 14 MILLION FANS SHOWED UP FOR TICKETS. EVENTUALLY TICKETMASTER HAD TO CANCEL THE PUBLIC SALE AS THERE WERE NO TICKETS LEFT. COMING UNDER MUCH CRITICISM FOR ITS FLAWED TICKETING SYSTEM, TICKETMASTER WAS EVEN SUED BY SOME CUSTOMERS WHILE LAW-MAKERS WERE SPURRED TO INVESTIGATE UNFAIR PRACTICES IN THE LIVE MUSIC PROMOTION BUSINESS. ONLY TAYLOR AND HER FANS COULD TURN A WEBSITE CRASH INTO A POLITICAL MOVEMENT.

Image: Barry King / Alamy Images

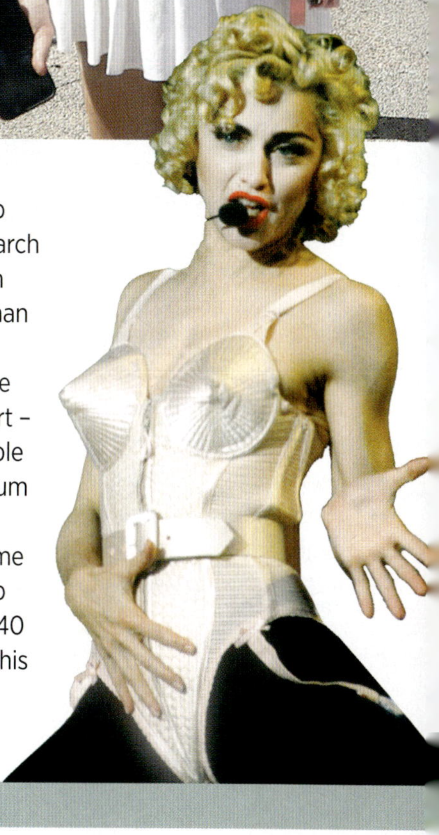

Taylor knocked Queen of Pop Madonna off her throne in March 2023, when she performed in Glendale, Arizona, to more than 69,000 fans. This broke the 'Vogue' singer's record for the most attended female concert – she had sung to 63,000 people in 1987 at the Anaheim Stadium in Germany. Taylor has also surpassed Madonna to become the woman with the most top tens in chart history, tallying 40 top ten hits in the Hot 100 – this is two more than Madonna.

Image: Gie Knaeps / Getty images

Continuing her reign as one of the most in-demand pop stars on the planet, Taylor broke world records when the Eras Tour sold over 2.4 million tickets on the first day of its presale alone. This was the most tickets sold by an artist in a single day, surpassing a record set by British singer Robbie Williams in 2005 with his Close Encounters Tour.

Image: John Medina / Getty images

The reputation Stadium Tour in 2018 made Taylor the female record holder for the highest-grossing tour in the United States. Yet forecasts predict her Eras Tour will outgross this, with the US leg alone projected to generate an estimated $591 million. This means Taylor is on track to beat Madonna's record to become the highest grossing female touring artist of all time – something the 'Material Girl' singer achieved with her Sweet & Sticky tour in 2009.

Image: Don Arnold / TAS18 / Getty images

There is surely no bigger pop sensation than The Beatles, but in 2021, Taylor undid a 54-year record set by the band when she dropped *Fearless (Taylor's Version)*. It was the third number-one album the singer scored in under a year, following the release of *evermore* and *folklore*. Having three chart-topping albums within 259 days of each other, she overtook The Beatles' record of 364 days, something they achieved with the albums *Help!*, *Rubber Sole* and *Revolver*.

Image: Fox Photos / Getty images

Track four on Taylor's album *Midnights* features the melodic vocals of Lana Del Rey. Called 'Snow On The Beach', the acoustic track broke Spotify records when the album was released for the most streams in a single week for an all-female collaboration. The singers photographed here at an awards ceremony in Germany in 2012 have been friends for years, but this was their first duet.

Image: Kevin Mazur / WireImage / Getty images

FRIENDLY COMPETITION BETWEEN THE CITIES SHE TOURED TO RESULTED IN CREATIVE WAYS TO HONOUR THE SINGER

Fun Fact

THE ERAS TOUR HAS ALSO PROVEN THE HUGE IMPACT TAYLOR CAN HAVE ON THE PLACES SHE VISITS. FRIENDLY COMPETITION BETWEEN THE CITIES SHE TOURED TO RESULTED IN EVER-MORE CREATIVE WAYS TO HONOUR THE SINGER. IT BEGAN WITH GLENDALE, WHICH TEMPORARILY CHANGED ITS NAME TO SWIFT CITY WHEN IT HOSTED THE FIRST TWO SHOWS OF THE TOUR. THEN ARLINGTON IN TEXAS RENAMED THE STREET OUTSIDE THE STADIUM TO TAYLOR SWIFT WAY FOR 24 HOURS TO CELEBRATE THE SINGER'S PERFORMANCE THERE, WHILE TAMPA IN FLORIDA INVITED TAYLOR TO BECOME AN HONORARY MAYOR FOR THE DAY AND NRG STADIUM IN TEXAS WAS TEMPORARILY RENAMED 'NRG STADIUM (TAYLOR'S VERSION)'.

Image: John Medina / Getty Images

EVERMORE

FASHION ICON, FILMMAKER AND FORCE FOR GOOD: TAYLOR WILL BE REMEMBERED FOR MORE THAN JUST HER MUSIC

JUST AS TAYLOR'S MUSIC EVOLVES WITH EVERY NEW ALBUM, SO DOES HER STYLE

For the *Fearless* section of the Eras setlist, Taylor channelled her second studio album by stepping out in a re-imagination of her iconic glittered fringe dress, complete with a rhinestone guitar. The outfit is part of a Swarovski crystal-embellished capsule collection designed by luxe Italian fashion brand, Roberto Cavalli.

Image: Kevin Winter / Getty images

Just as Taylor's music evolves with every new album, so does her style. This was proved during the Eras Tour when her outfits changed multiple times throughout the set to reflect each of her ten musical eras. Here she performs the acoustic section on the opening night wearing a ruffled Jessica Jones gown, reminiscent of her early days of curls, cowboy boots and flowing dresses.

Image: Kevin Mazur / Getty images

With 'We are never getting back together like ever' emblazoned across her Ashish t-shirt, there's no doubt Taylor is celebrating her *RED* album. The slogan changed most tour dates, but the fedora hat always stayed the same – a throwback to the preppy look of stripes, varsity jackets and short shorts she worked back on The RED Tour in 2013.

Image: Omar Vega / TAS23 / Getty images

TAYLOR CHANNELLED HER SECOND ALBUM WITH A RE-IMAGINATION OF HER GLITTERED FRINGE DRESS, COMPLETE WITH A RHINESTONE GUITAR

Capturing the fairy-tale romance of her third album, *Speak Now*, Taylor stepped out to perform 'Enchanted' to a Tampa, Florida crowd wearing a beautiful Elie Saab haute couture gown with floral tulle detailing. It can be considered a more grown-up version of the now-iconic gold Valentino dress she wore during the Speak Now Tour back in 2012.

Image: Octavio Jones / TAS23 / Getty images

Did you know?

WHEN AN 18-YEAR-OLD BILLIE EILISH WON ALBUM OF THE YEAR FOR *WHEN WE ALL FALL ASLEEP, WHERE DO WE GO?* AT THE 2020 GRAMMY AWARDS, SHE BROKE TAYLOR'S RECORD FOR BEING THE YOUNGEST EVER ARTIST TO TAKE HOME THE HIGHLY COVETED AWARD. BUT THERE IS A LOT OF LOVE BETWEEN THE TWO STARS, WITH BILLIE FANGIRLING OVER OLD-SCHOOL TAYLOR SONGS AND ACKNOWLEDGING HOW THE OLDER SINGER'S EFFORTS TO CALL OUT MALE PRIVILEGE IN THE MUSIC INDUSTRY HAS POSITIVELY IMPACTED HER OWN JOURNEY IN THE BUSINESS. TAYLOR RETURNED THE ADORATION BY SAYING BILLIE WAS ONE OF THE MOST INFLUENTIAL FEMALE POP ARTISTS.

Image: Kevin Mazur / Getty Images

Taylor opened The Eras Tour each night wearing different variations of a rainbow-hued Atelier Versace bodysuit, referencing the dreamy pastel aesthetic of her *Lover* album. To perform 'The Man', she pulled on this sequined pinstripe Versace blazer over the top for a fiercer vibe befitting of the feminist anthem.

Image: Octavio Jones / TAS23 / Getty images

The most dramatic look of The Eras Tour was easily Roberto Cavalli's one-legged jumpsuit. The design featured a three-dimensional, embroidered snake motif winding from Taylor's ankle to the top of her leg, leaving nobody guessing she was in *reputation* era mode. While touring this album in 2018, the set featured a huge python in response to Kim Kardashian's online name calling.

Image: Terence Rushin / TAS23 / Getty images

WHILE TOURING IN 2018, THE SET FEATURED A HUGE PYTHON IN RESPONSE TO KIM KARDASHIAN'S ONLINE NAME CALLING

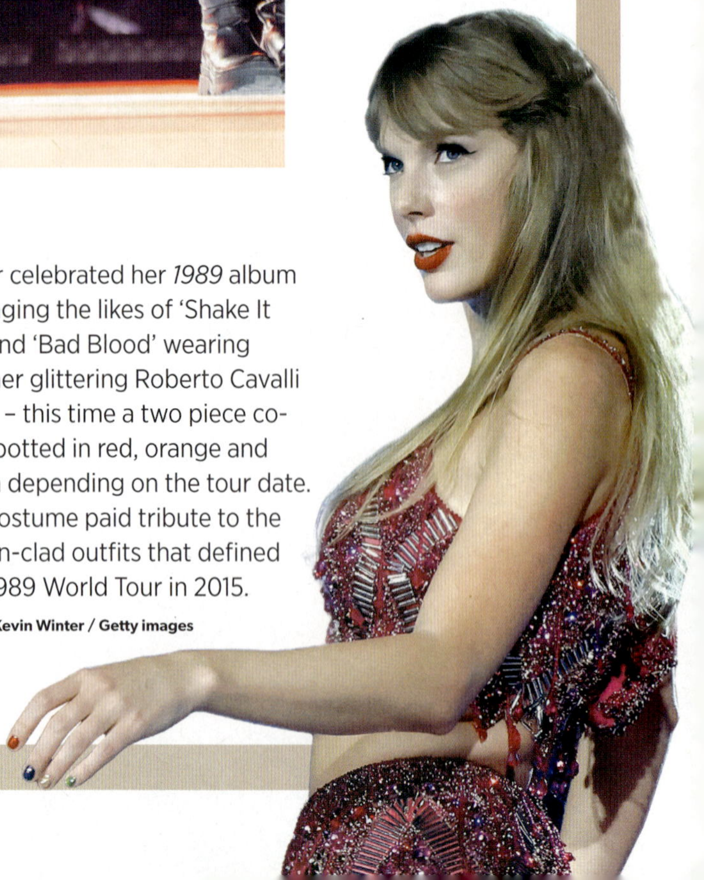

Taylor celebrated her *1989* album by singing the likes of 'Shake It Off' and 'Bad Blood' wearing another glittering Roberto Cavalli outfit – this time a two piece co-ord spotted in red, orange and green depending on the tour date. The costume paid tribute to the sequin-clad outfits that defined The 1989 World Tour in 2015.

Image: Kevin Winter / Getty images

Lace, plaid and a red lip will forever be associated with Taylor's *evermore* album and she brought the cottage core styling to the stage by wearing a whimsical orange prairie dress complete with a ruffled, embroidered bodice. Referencing the nature imagery present throughout the 15 album tracks, she even performed on a moss-covered piano.

Image: Kevin Winter / Getty images

Rounding off the three-hour-long setlist with tracks from *Midnights*, Taylor closed the show on opening night wearing this midnight blue leotard designed by Oscar de la Renta. The aesthetic of the 2022 album is heavily 1970s-influenced, from the autumnal palette of the record's artwork to shimmering disco pizazz, as exemplified by this retro-glam outfit.

Image: Kevin Mazur / Getty images

Wearing a delicate chiffon Alberta Ferretti gown, Taylor was in full folksy mode when singing her ethereal melodies from *folklore*. The cosy cabin in the woods she dreamt up while writing the album in lockdown made it into the set, reminding us of how she managed to propel the prairie aesthetic into peak popularity.

Image: Ethan Miller / TAS23 / Getty images

THE COSY CABIN IN THE WOODS SHE DREAMT UP WHILE WRITING THE ALBUM IN LOCKDOWN MADE IT INTO THE SET

On another performance of 'The Man', Taylor strutted her stuff in this silver-clad Versace blazer. The song marked a pivotal point for the singer when it was released, as it was the first track she solo directed a music video for. She has since directed the music videos for 'Cardigan', 'Willow', 'Anti-Hero', 'Bejewelled' as well as 'Lavender Haze'.

Image: John Medina / Stringer / Getty images

From directing music videos to making her own short films, Taylor is certainly expanding her skillset and picking up awards in the process. *All Too Well: A Short Film* racked up an American Music Award, a Grammy and a Hollywood Critics Award. She also brought a whole new level of publicity to the Toronto International Film Festival, where Swifties camped out overnight to catch a glimpse of the singer on the red carpet ahead of a screening of the film.

Image: VALERIE MACON / AFP / Getty images

Proving herself to be a creative powerhouse, Taylor was also the subject of *Miss Americana*, a 2020 documentary film following the singer over the course of several years. It takes place during a transitional phase of her career as she wraps up the 2018 Reputation Stadium Tour and begins creating her album, *Lover*. This still from the Netflix documentary shows the star backstage, prepping for her appearance on the 2019 MTV Video Music Awards.

Image: Ron Harvey / Getty images

Dressed in a Carmen March houndstooth jumpsuit, Taylor attends the *Miss Americana* premiere at the 2020 Sundance Film Festival. Critics have praised the documentary for the 'emotional heft' of Taylor's interviews, which discussed issues including eating disorders, self-esteem and sexual assault. There was an unprecedented surge in attendees at the festival and increased media coverage thanks to Taylor's presence.

Image: Neilson Barnard / Getty images

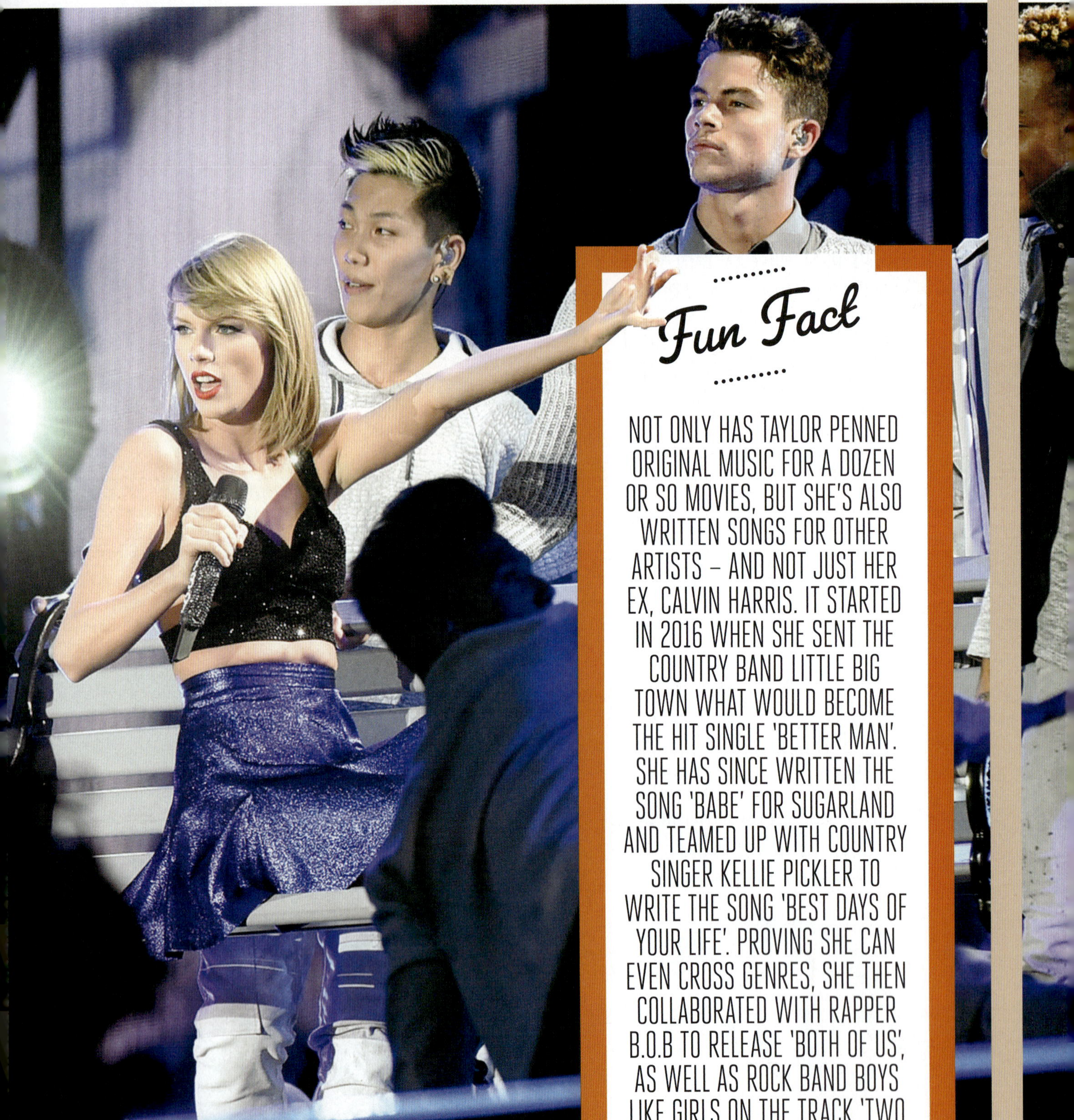

Fun Fact

NOT ONLY HAS TAYLOR PENNED ORIGINAL MUSIC FOR A DOZEN OR SO MOVIES, BUT SHE'S ALSO WRITTEN SONGS FOR OTHER ARTISTS – AND NOT JUST HER EX, CALVIN HARRIS. IT STARTED IN 2016 WHEN SHE SENT THE COUNTRY BAND LITTLE BIG TOWN WHAT WOULD BECOME THE HIT SINGLE 'BETTER MAN'. SHE HAS SINCE WRITTEN THE SONG 'BABE' FOR SUGARLAND AND TEAMED UP WITH COUNTRY SINGER KELLIE PICKLER TO WRITE THE SONG 'BEST DAYS OF YOUR LIFE'. PROVING SHE CAN EVEN CROSS GENRES, SHE THEN COLLABORATED WITH RAPPER B.O.B TO RELEASE 'BOTH OF US', AS WELL AS ROCK BAND BOYS LIKE GIRLS ON THE TRACK 'TWO IS BETTER THAN ONE'.

Image: Jason Merritt / Getty Images

Did you know?

TAYLOR IS AS MUCH A FORCE ON TIKTOK AS SHE IS IN MUSIC. HER UBER-LOYAL FANS HAVE BEEN CULTIVATING A FEVERED COLLECTIVE ON THE PLATFORM KNOWN AS SWIFTTOK, WHERE THEY GO TO RANK HER SONGS, REVIEW HER ALBUMS AND SHOW OFF THEIR VINYL. IN FACT, THE ONLINE COMMUNITY DISSECTS EVERY MOVE THE SINGER MAKES WITH LABORATORY PRECISION. FROM MERCH RELEASES AND RED CARPET APPEARANCES, TO SOCIAL MEDIA POSTS AND MUSIC VIDEOS – NO ACTION IS IGNORED AS SWIFTIES CLAMBER TO PREDICT TAYLOR'S NEXT STEPS. THIS IS JUST ANOTHER EXAMPLE OF HOW TAYLOR'S FANBASE IS AMONG THE MOST DEVOTED IN THE WORLD.

Image: Jun Sato / TAS18 / Getty Images

Taylor wrote and directed a documentary concert film called *folklore: The Long Pond Studio Sessions*, available to watch on Disney Plus. In the programme, Taylor performs all 17 tracks of her eighth album, *folklore*, while discussing the creative process and inspiration behind the songs with her co-producers Aaron Dessner and Jack Antonoff.

Image: Everett Collection / Alamy images

After a small role in dystopian sci-fi movie *The Giver*, Taylor took a five-year acting hiatus before returning to filmdom in 2019 as Bombalurina in *Cats* – the movie adaption of Andrew Lloyd Webber's stage musical of the same name. Starring alongside big names including Jennifer Hudson, Judi Dench, James Corden and Rebel Wilson, she penned an original number for the film called 'Beautiful Ghosts' which went on to receive a Grammy nomination.

Image: Taylor Hill / FilmMagic / Getty images

The pop star is no stranger to the silver screen either. In 2012, she voiced the character Audrey in Dr Seuss' *The Lorax* – the CGI animated film starring Zac Efron and Danny DeVito. But it was not her first acting role. A big *CSI* fan, she had played a rebellious teenager in one episode of the crime drama in 2009 and made her feature film debut in 2010 in the romcom *Valentine's Day*.

Image: Kevin Winter / Getty images

Whether it's standing up to industry bullies or fighting for ownership of her own songs, Taylor has long been paving the way for women in the music industry. Among the younger generation of female artists who cite the singer-songwriter as an inspiration are Olivia Rodrigo, Maisie Peters, Phoebe Bridgers and Gayle, seen here opening for Taylor on The Eras Tour.

Image: Omar Vega / TAS23 / Getty images

More recently you might have spotted Taylor on the promotional posters for the 1930s-set mystery thriller, *Amsterdam*. Playing the character Elizabeth Meekins, she shares the credits of the 2022 film with a long list of Hollywood stalwarts such as Margot Robbie, Christian Bale, Anya Taylor-Joy, Rami Malek and Robert De Niro.

Image: Everett Collection / Alamy images

Fun Fact

TAYLOR'S MOVIE-MAKING SKILLS WILL BE COMING TO THE BIG SCREEN SOON, COURTESY OF AMERICAN STUDIO SEARCHLIGHT PICTURES. ALTHOUGH MANY DETAILS ABOUT TAYLOR'S FEATURE-LENGTH DIRECTIONAL DEBUT ARE BEING KEPT UNDER WRAPS, WE KNOW SHE HAS PENNED THE SCRIPT. "I'D LOVE TO KEEP TAKING BABY STEPS FORWARD," SHE SAID DURING A DISCUSSION AT THE 2022 TORONTO FILM FESTIVAL. "AND I THINK THAT I'M AT A PLACE NOW WHERE THE NEXT BABY STEP IS NOT A BABY STEP. IT WOULD BE COMMITTING TO MAKING A FILM. AND I FEEL LIKE I WOULD JUST ABSOLUTELY LOVE FOR THE RIGHT OPPORTUNITY TO ARISE BECAUSE I JUST ABSOLUTELY, ABSOLUTELY ADORE TELLING STORIES THIS WAY."

Image: Bob Levey / TAS23 / Getty Images

Taylor is not just making an impact on upcoming names in the music industry. She is also behind what guitar manufacturer Fender terms the 'Taylor Swift factor' – the phenomenon of rising guitar sales among women. Originally thought to be a short-term spike, the singer's influence was underestimated, as females continue to drive sales and actually make up half of those who are learning to play the instrument.

Image: Octavio Jones / TAS23 / Getty images

Did you know?

IT'S ALREADY COMMON KNOWLEDGE THAT TAYLOR WROTE THE ORIGINAL SONG 'CAROLINA' FOR THE 2022 FILM ADAPTATION OF *WHERE THE CRAWDADS SING*. BUT FEW REALISE THE IDEA WAS ENTIRELY THE SINGER'S OWN. AFTER FALLING IN LOVE WITH THE BOOK BY DELIA OWENS A FEW YEARS AGO, SHE PENNED THE NEW PIECE OF MUSIC AS SOON SHE HEARD REESE WITHERSPOON WAS PRODUCING THE MOVIE VERSION AND IT WAS GOING TO STAR BRITISH ACTRESS DAISY EDGAR-JONES. "I WANTED TO CREATE SOMETHING HAUNTING AND ETHEREAL TO MATCH THIS MESMERISING STORY," SWIFT SAID. LUCKILY REESE AND HER TEAM WERE OVERJOYED, SAYING THEY WERE "THE BENEVOLENT RECEIVERS OF [AN] INCREDIBLE ARTISTIC GIFT".

Image: Album / Alamy Images

In the midst of re-recording her first six albums, Taylor is gradually reclaiming control over the music she has created and single-handedly reshaping the way wealth is distributed in the industry. By upending the system, she is paving the way for other artists to do the same and proving herself to be an invaluable change-marker along the way.

Image: Bob Levey / TAS23 / Getty images

A perfect example of Taylor's marketing genius is how she kept fans hooked in the lead-up to the release of *Midnights*. After taking to Instagram Live to describe the forthcoming record, she posted a series of videos on TikTok titled 'Midnights mayhem with me' where she used a bingo cage to randomly select one song off the 13-track album and announce its title. She also worked with Spotify to release lyric snippets on billboards around the world, catering to all her global fanbase.

Image: Hazel Plater / Alamy images

EVERMORE

As well as being one of the best song-writers and performers on the planet, Taylor's marketing game is also up there with the best. From writing intimate blogs on Myspace and Tumblr, to breadcrumbing her Twitter and Instagram followers ahead of album releases, she has used social media to stay connected to her fans in a way no other pop star has been able to replicate.

Image: PjrStudio / Alamy images

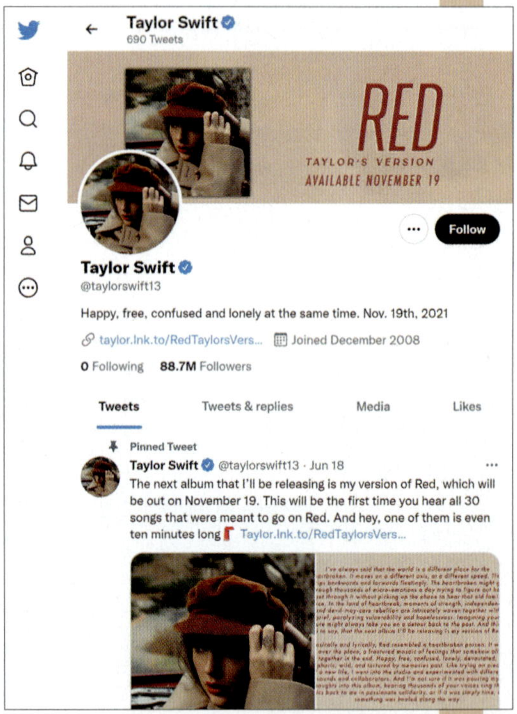

SHE HAS USED SOCIAL MEDIA TO STAY CONNECTED TO HER FANS IN A WAY NO OTHER POP STAR HAS BEEN ABLE TO

ULTIMATE 90s POP COLLECTION
CELEBRATING THE SONGS & SOUNDS OF THE GREATEST DECADE IN MUSIC
BRITPOP • SOUNDTRACKS • BOY BANDS
Celebrate the songs and sounds of the greatest decades in music
PROG COLLECTION
The Complete Story YES
MILEY CYRUS FANBOOK
CLASSIC ROCK ICONS of Rock'n'Roll
The story of BOB MARLEY
The complete story of the pioneering reggae superstar
ALL THE CLASSICS
LIFE & LEGACY
THE UNTOLD STORY
MARILLION
HARRY STYLES FANBOOK
GUNS N' ROSES
Explore the lives and legacies of some of the world's most iconic artists
The Ultimate 70s Collection
NEW! ROCK HAMMER PRESENT IRON MAIDEN
THE COMPLETE STORY
EXCLUSIVE INTERVIEWS!
50 GREATEST SONGS!
EVERY MAIDEN ALBUM in their own words!
ABBEY ROAD
THE ULTIMATE BEATLES COLLECTION
McCARTNEY
A LIFE'S WORK
Crank up the volume and get to know the best rock and metal bands on the planet
QUEEN
PINK FLOYD
Get great savings when you buy direct from us
1000s of great titles, many not available anywhere else
World-wide delivery and super-safe ordering